Cal Turner Jr

• *Praise for* LED TO FOLLOW •

"**LED TO FOLLOW** is a small package of dynamite for your business and personal log jams!...Taking conventional leadership to a higher level, their formula defines success worth having as **FOLLOWERSHIP**."
> – DAVE RAMSEY, National Radio and TV Talk-Show
> Host, and Author

"Howard Olds is one of the most effective pastor/leaders I know. Cal Turner has proven himself as a leader in the business world. Their partnership of sharing in this volume is a unique contribution to those who would be leaders. It is sound in leadership principles, grounded in practice, and flavored with rich experience and commitment. I wish I could have learned from these friends forty years ago."
> – MAXIE DUNNAM, Chancellor,
> Asbury Theological Seminary

"**LED TO FOLLOW** is an engaging, thought-provoking and inspiring book that challenges readers to become leaders who are truly worth following. . . . As my good friend and an exceptional volunteer leader for the Y, Cal has lived out the truths in this book by demonstrating the ability and willingness to help lead our organization with a strong moral compass. This book is a treasure, a blessing, and a great resource for any leader or aspiring leader."
> – JOHN MARK "JOURNEY" JOHNSON, President and CEO,
> YMCA of Middle Tennessee

"These two admirable leaders know the secret of leadership success. People don't follow leaders because they are forced to, but because they trust their leader knows where they are going and will take care of them along the way. Olds and Turner are personal, transparent, and wise leaders to follow."
> – JAMES HUDNUT-BEUMLER, Dean of Vanderbilt
> Divinity School

continued next page

"A minister who manages and a manager who ministers… combine their ideas and experiences to give us some keen insights about leadership that are as fresh as the morning sun and as time-honored as the Bible. I commend this book to you highly!"

> – JAMES W. MOORE, Author of *Jesus' Parables About Making Choices* and *Faith Is the Answer, but What Are the Questions?*

"Remarkable leaders themselves, Howard Olds and Cal Turner Jr. provide significant insight, wisdom, and guidance for other leaders…. They display the wonderful fruit that emerges when outstanding business leaders and gifted pastors nurture each other's vocations."

> – L. GREGORY JONES, Dean of Duke Divinity School

"This book was written to disturb our collective soul. An inability to follow always means an incapacity to lead well. The authors make character front and center and do so in such a way that it makes me want to be a follower that people can lead and a leader that people can follow."

> – DR. JOHN JACKSON, Author of *Leveraging Your Leadership Style* and *Pastorpreneur*, www.pastorpreneur.com

"Cal Turner and Howard Olds have been leaders in our church for a long time. Now these proven leaders teach us how to be better followers and, by implication, how to be more faithful leaders."

> – WILLIAM H. WILLIMON, Resident Bishop Birmingham Area, The United Methodist Church

"With personal vulnerability and vocational passion, a faithful pastor and a committed CEO… share wit and wisdom gleaned from their own faith and experiences and the result is a helpful resource for persons who seek to be faithful and effective participants in God's mission through the church and in the world."

> – BISHOP KENNETH L. CARDER, Ruth W. and A. Morris Williams, Jr., Professor of the Practice of Christian Ministry

LED TO
FOLLOW

LED TO FOLLOW

LEADERSHIP LESSONS
FROM AN
IMPROBABLE PASTOR
AND A
RELUCTANT CEO

J. HOWARD OLDS
& CAL TURNER JR.

Abingdon Press
Nashville

LED TO FOLLOW: LEADERSHIP LESSONS FROM AN IMPROBABLE PASTOR AND A RELUCTANT CEO

Copyright © 2008 by Abingdon Press

All rights reserved.

This book is printed on acid-free paper.

Library of Congress Cataloging-in-Publication Data

Olds, J. Howard.
Led to follow : leadership lessons from am improbable pastor and a reluctant CEO / J. Howard Olds and Cal Turner.
    p.   cm.
ISBN 978-0-687-65079-8 (binding: hardback with dust cover : alk. paper)
1. Christian leadership—Methodist church.   I. Turner, Cal.   II. Title.
BX8349.L43043 2008
253—dc22

2007049179

Scripture quotations unless otherwise indicated are from the New Revised Standard Version of the Bible, copyright 1989, Division of Christian Education of the National Council of Churches of Christ in the United States of America. Used by permission. All rights reserved.

Scripture marked NIV is taken from the Holy Bible, NEW INTERNATIONAL VERSION®. Copyright © 1973, 1978, 1984 by International Bible Society. All rights reserved throughout the world. Used by permission of International Bible Society.

Scripture marked KJV is from the King James or Authorized Version of the Bible.

08 09 10 11 12 13 14 15 16 17—10 9 8 7 6 5 4 3 2 1

MANUFACTURED IN THE UNITED STATES OF AMERICA

ACKNOWLEDGMENTS

First I want to thank Bob Spain for sharing my *Faith Breaks*, which generated interest from John Kutsko. I want to thank John for proposing this idea of a joint venture and his patience as we tested the concept. I want to thank Rob Simbeck for his assistance writing this manuscript. We could not have completed this adventure without his help. Thanks to our editor, Jessica Kelley, for taking on the impossible task of pulling all these ideas together into readable form. A special thanks to Carla Barrios, my administrative assistant, for her tireless work with manuscripts. And I want to thank my wife, Sandy, for her encouragement, along with all the people of Brentwood United Methodist Church for their unending support. And last but not least, thanks to Cal Turner Jr., for agreeing to make this journey with me. It's been fun.

—J. Howard Olds

I thank God for Howard Olds. I am blessed to have had the loving friendship of a pastor who can actually open up as a real person to a backslider in his flock! This book has been hard for me to write, but Howard has inspired me to be focused and disciplined.

I am also grateful to Rob Simbeck, who just might be the best follower of all in this book on followership. Rob has been able to follow what I am feeling and thinking and get it into print far better than I ever could have without him.

In addition to being blessed by many loving relationships of family and friends, I am also thankful for the humble old farmer who bought a pair of thirty-nine-cent panties from me at Allen Dry Goods in Scottsville, Kentucky, in 1953. Though I never knew his name, he greatly affected my life by helping me have a bigger heart for serving the wonderful low- and fixed-income clientele of Dollar General Corporation.

—Cal Turner Jr.

CONTENTS

CHAPTER 1

FOLLOWING:
A NEW UNDERSTANDING

Leadership for a large part means to be led.
Henri Nouwen

It is often said that unless you are the lead dog pulling the sled, the scenery never changes. Neither, we could add, does the smell.

There, in a nutshell, lies our problem with following. We like neither the look nor the smell of it. Ask the contestants on *American Idol*, *The Apprentice*, or *Survivor*. Ask the athletes using chemical means to enhance performance. Ask the executives willing to do anything to boost quarterly numbers. No one is scrambling for the chance to yell, "We're Number 7!"

How many times have we heard, "If you want to be somebody, become a leader"? Dare to challenge that outlook by noting that leaders require followers, and the reply is always swift and certain: "Well, I know which position *I* prefer."

It should be no surprise, then, that there are plenty of books on leadership. The average bookstore can inundate you with them. Politicians like Rudy Giuliani and corporate executives like Jack Welch share their experiences and life lessons. Coaches like John Wooden and Rick Pitino tell people how to succeed using the principles of sports. Entrepreneur pastors like Bill Hybels encourage clergy to be courageous leaders.

The most popular of them all is minister-turned-businessman John Maxwell, who cranks out long lists of irrefutable laws and indispensable qualities related to leadership. His most recent title, *The 360° Leader*, bolsters a long-held suspicion that leaders really do spend a lot of time running around in circles.

All of these books are helpful—there *are* tried and true principles that separate success from failure and winners from losers—and many of us have benefited greatly from reading and applying their teachings. These leadership principles, however, generally focus on the self, on personal skills and traits to be cultivated, when true leadership requires looking beyond our own capabilities to something greater than ourselves. Such leadership goes beyond simply putting others' needs before our own. In the thirty years since Robert Greenleaf gave the world his book *Servant Leadership*, many politicians, pastors, CEOs, and athletes have stumbled and fallen. A president has been impeached. High-profile preachers have gone to prison. Sports heroes have found themselves in court. Television personalities like Martha Stewart have been convicted of wrongdoing. Executives at Enron have brought about the biggest corporate failure in United States history. Too often we have seen leaders betray their trust, embarrass themselves, and, in the case of Enron, cost others millions of dollars in lost revenue and retirement benefits.

These leaders did not slip and fall because of their lack of knowledge. They knew how to run companies, lead governments, develop churches, and win ball games. But something was missing! Beautifully rigged ships with broken rudders will run aground. Expensively mounted political campaigns flounder for a moment's lapse in moral judgment. And talented, charismatic leaders can waste promise and opportunity if they operate with an incomplete view of leadership. It is this missing ingredient that we propose to address in this book.

We believe this ingredient is *followership*—the ability and willingness to follow something greater than ourselves. Just as leadership is more than mere leading, followership is a calling higher than simply following another leader. Rather, it is leadership with a moral compass, guided by the magnetic north of mission and bound by empathy and mutual respect for those with whom it shares the journey. It follows a powerful vision and embraces the unpredictability of life and work.

On the surface, leading by following couldn't seem like more of an oxymoron—an apparently incongruous phrase like jumbo shrimp, civil war, old news, or even United Methodists—but can anyone lead who is not willing to follow? Can a leader who honors no calling higher than his or her own objectives truly inspire and influence others to greatness? Do leaders fail because they refuse to follow?

Follow may not be a very popular word, but here's the truth—all great leaders are great followers! It was true of Moses, of Paul, of Winston Churchill, of Nelson Mandela. These were people whose charisma was more a product of the purity of their vision, of their ability to hold fast to a cause, than of any talent or skill they had developed. They are examples of the fact that we are talking about an elevated form of following, one that qualifies us for true leadership.

Followership is more attitude than action, more "being" than "doing," a matter of the heart as well as a decision of the head. We tend to measure people by what they do or fail to do. Accomplishment is the name of the game in business, in sports, and yes, even in the church. But what if our successes or failures, our accomplishments or hesitations, our actions or inactions, come from a deeper, more obscure part of our personhood? What if our "being" *determines* our "doing"? If this is the case, if leadership is more a matter of who we are than what we do, then we must look deeper into our souls to find the essence of leadership. We must find and follow the things that will lead us to a life of mission and fulfillment.

We might ask ourselves questions like these:

- What is my core identity as a person?
- What is my purpose for being?
- Am I willing to learn from others, and to share credit and control?
- How can I best handle failure?
- Am I able to adapt to changing circumstances?
- Do I seek wisdom by finding answers, or by asking the right questions and living with confidence even when there are no clear answers?

Thoughtful responses to these questions, which we will address in the coming chapters, help lay a foundation on which a life of followership might be built. It is a process that demands much of us, for to lead we must follow our true selves; our mission; the people we hope to serve; the faults, failures, and changes that come with life; and yes, even the questions that have no easy answers. Followership relies on unshakable core values and personal integrity, and a life purpose to which the leader is truly dedicated. Flaws in those underlying structures will always show through.

The true leader draws from a deep sense of calling and purpose, staying focused on the mission, while also listening to the people sharing the path and supporting the mission. The result is truly inspirational leadership that is as individual as the time and place it inhabits, and yet as universally recognizable as the quality, integrity, and charisma that infuse it.

Bosses and managers can be faceless, wishy-washy, interchangeable. The leader immersed in the principles of followership will be anything but. It's the difference between the faceless bureaucrat and the spellbinding orator, between the sycophantic courtier and the spirited coach. Sometimes its approach is quiet and deliberate, and sometimes it is impassioned and energetic, but always it is purposeful and potent. Followership is Moses smashing tablets, John calling out in the wilderness, Winston Churchill's "blood, toil, tears, and sweat" speech, Nelson Mandela's long stint in that South African jail cell. Forget bleating sheep. Think noble ram.

Followership is about being tuned-in to group creativity and strength, about recognizing and drawing out the best in other people in light of the vision at hand, whether it is winning a ball game, inspiring a nation to a great cause, or simply living a life of integrity and selflessness. It is about neither ego-driven will nor being led by the mob. It is walking with others on a path guided by a shining star and made smooth by mutual inspiration. Its communication is based on respect of others, empathy for them, and genuine dialogue with them.

In this book, we will discuss the nature and practical application of followership, not with empirical data or rigid steps to follow, but with the experiences and insights of real people who struggle to lead from within. To begin, consider the stories of an admired modern-day general and of an itinerant preacher regarded by many as the greatest leader to ever walk the earth.

The military is full of people following orders, but at least one modern military hero seems to have made following his calling and his colleagues a vital part of his leadership. For his book *American Generalship*, Edgar Puryear Jr. asked Colin Powell why he believed he was selected to be chairman of the Joint Chiefs of Staff. Powell replied:

> I was very loyal to people who appointed me, people who were under me, and my associates. I developed a reputation as somebody you could trust. I would give you my very, very best. I would always try to do what I thought was right and I let the chips fall where they might. . . . It didn't really make a difference whether I made general in terms of my self-respect and self-esteem. I just loved being in the army.[1]

Powell led by following his passion for the military, his personal integrity, and his respect for his colleagues. He relied not on his own charisma or talent, but followed values greater than he, becoming a leader whom others could not help following.

Nearly two billion people claim to be followers of Jesus Christ. Over 80 percent of Americans consider themselves Christians. Nonetheless, even those among us who are lifelong students of the life and teachings of Jesus can still be captured by the simplicity and directness of his call. It consisted of these compelling words: "Follow me!" He issued that invitation to fishermen and tax collectors, homemakers and prostitutes, high-profile officials and leprous beggars. The amazing thing is that people readily answered that call and followed Jesus. Immediately, without hesitation, they left their nets and their places of business, their families and their friends, and followed. They did not know where they were going or how they would get there. They just followed! What caused them to go so quickly? What did this Master Teacher touch in the human spirit that stimulated that kind of devotion?

From beginning to end, it's plain that this carpenter from Nazareth was a follower too. He followed his heavenly Father, his unique identity, and his redemptive purpose for being on earth in the first place. He resisted the temptation of stardom that causes so many to stumble. He could handle criticism and defeat without compromising his personhood. He lived with questions that he continued to ask all the way to his death. One cannot study his life without sensing that he was clearly a man on a mission, following a calling far bigger than his own immediate gratification. Still today, people feel compelled to follow this great follower.

BECOMING A LEADER WORTH FOLLOWING

With examples as illustrious as Jesus Christ, we may ask what followers today look like. What are the character traits that enable a leader to be a true follower? To name a few of the obvious ones: Great followers have a **teachable** spirit. They are humble. They know that they do not know it all. Followers are willing to learn from anyone, regardless of stature. They are not afraid to ask probing, insightful questions. They use their mistakes as learning tools. They are willing to try new ideas and distill the insights for the benefit of all. Of course, such openness requires a sturdy self-identity and a strong identification with the common mission.

Disciple is a word seldom used in our time, but it is a good word for people with these traits. A disciple is a student, a learner, and, yes, a follower. Disciples do not always get it right the first time, often making the same mistakes over and over, but disciples keep coming back until they do get it right. Jesus called twelve men to be his disciples. While there were a good many more followers and admirers, these twelve were often taken away for special training and instruction. Did they fail? Did they misunderstand? Were they afraid? Of course! Yet Jesus entrusted the continuation of his whole mission on earth to these twelve teachable followers, who in turn became leaders of the original Christian community of 120, which in turn grew into the millions of people who follow the Christian faith today.

Great followers are also **trustworthy**. They are dependable, reliable, loyal, and faithful to the end. They can keep a confidence. They can achieve a goal. They are willing to take responsibility. Trust is a precious commodity. It is never automatic, but must be built gradually. While a boss can command unquestioned authority, the true leader will earn the trust of those he or she is leading.

Great followers are **truthful**. Truth, of course, is more than mere gossip, and truth is more than stating facts. Facts can be cold, hard, and brutal; so we are instructed to speak the truth in love. Truth might be defined as the purposeful selection of relevant, appropriately actionable facts. Aristotle urged people to speak the right truth to the right person at the right time for the right reason in the right way. Simply telling people what you think they want to hear is helpful neither to the receiver nor to the giver. We will talk more about communication in chapter 4, but the importance of honest dialogue between leaders and those carrying out the mission cannot be overstated.

Great followers are **tenacious**. They are willing to do whatever it takes to get the job done right. Followers do not quit in the face of struggle or turmoil. They are not defeated by detours and delays. They treat dead ends as opportunities for new ideas. Commitment is a great mainsail in a sea of uncertainty. We cannot control the weather, world events, personal troubles, community change, or the stock market. We can only control what we do with the situation as it is. The problem with life is that it has an "if" right in the middle of it. Life is "iffy," but we don't have to be. Tenacity calls us to be there regardless of the weather, the woes, the weariness, or even the wars of life. Great leaders will follow their vision and circumstances no matter how difficult the road may become.

Last, great followers are **team players**. They know it's the team that deserves and gets the credit. Great followers share the spotlight. The University of Florida Gators won rare back-to-back NCAA basketball championships in 2006 and 2007. Now, sports commentators like to enumerate the attributes of great coaches and name star players for each game. Sports fans love heroes. But as the championship Gators cut down the nets in celebration of their victory, analysts struggled to name an individual star player. The Florida Gators did not have the best players in college basketball. They had the best *team* in college basketball.

All of us would be wise to take that team concept to work with us each day. Superstars alone do not win championships or build great businesses. It takes teamwork to get the job done. Anything less is not enough. Teamwork assumes mutual responsibility and accountability. Ideas come from everybody. So do credit and criticism. The name of the game is cooperation, not competition.

Now, speaking of teamwork, you might think that a minister and a businessman make a rather odd couple. Why should a clergyman and a retired CEO try to write a book together? That question is something we have pondered many times. It helps that we have become friends through the process of sharing the lifetime of experiences that have shaped us. We have talked about the good and the bad, the high points and the struggles, the things that have improved us and those which nearly derailed us.

As we shared, we also discovered how much our respective vocations overlapped. One of us is a minister who manages, and the other is a manager who ministers. We recognized first that whether we are leading a business or a church, our successes or failures are tied directly to the personal values and core convictions we bring to the table. We are what we follow! Refined techniques and high-tech operations can never replace the soul of a person. We agreed that churches can benefit from the wisdom of business, and business can learn from the mission of the Church. Clergy are often more likely to read leadership books written by business gurus than by other clergy. Likewise, the phenomenal success of Pastor Rick Warren's *The Purpose Driven Life* is evidence that the secular world is starving for a purposeful life built on something other than materialistic, self-serving standards of success.

We wondered why churches, and particularly why denominations, have not adapted more business principles through the years. Our own denomination (The United Methodist Church) has 35,000 local churches scattered across the United States. We have CEOs in the form of bishops, and district managers in the form of district superintendents. We have regional distribution centers in the form of annual conferences. We have a corporate mission of making disciples of Jesus Christ. What could our denomination, or any denomination, learn from successful business models across the country? Could any business, for instance, ignore a 30 percent decline in its customer base, the kind the denomination has experienced in the last decades? What could we adapt in the form of core values, strategic planning, honest evaluations, and new strategies taken for granted in business?

Businesses, on the other hand, have much to learn from churches. The vision of Dollar General Corp. is "A Better Life For Everyone," and the mission is "serving others." Serving is a core value of this corporation. Churches have been in the serving business for two thousand years. Someone asked John Maxwell where he got all his leadership principles. John hesitated for a moment and then replied, "Everything I know, I learned from the Bible." Servant-leadership was a religious term long before it became a business term.

Then we looked to a still wider arena. In an age of cataclysmic social problems and declining government assistance in our country and around the world, the time may be right for religious groups, business corporations, and individuals to form teams capable of fighting disease, rebuilding neighborhoods, providing education, protecting children, and, most of all, restoring a sense of worth and dignity to a growing number of human beings who are devoid of hope. It will take creative, committed leaders to build these bridges. It will take leaders who are willing to follow their true God-given purposes. It will take people willing to fail and to learn as they go along, willing to ask the hard questions even when there are no known answers. That's what followership is all about, and it's what we'll be exploring in the pages of this book.

FROM THE DESK OF
CAL TURNER JR.

Throughout my career at Dollar General, I wrestled with un-certainty over what *true* leadership is, and how to practice it in our company, given the inherent limitations of my position as the boss's son. I joined the company in 1965, following in the foot-steps of my father and grandfather, and one of the challenges from the beginning was overcoming the style of leadership that I had inherited. It was apparent from early on that the manage-ment style of the previous generation would not be relevant to the future.

The word *president* used to stick in my throat when I intro-duced myself—I didn't want to be a "boss" in the traditional sense. We had to move from bossism to leadership. Leaders have to "get over themselves," and I had to get over being the boss's son. Our management team had its own challenges, its own barriers to leadership. They would have to get over putting me in a boss's cocoon while putting themselves down in the sub-servient ways typical of an entrepreneurial organization. They were going to need to step up to the plate. I had to convince them that I really wanted them to tell the truth as *they* saw it, and that the greatest truth would be what we discovered together from our customers. In a retail company, that is where the real authority should lie—with the customer. If the company responds to the customers and the leader responds to employees, suc-cess is assured.

I had always heard my dad and grandfather agree that low-end retailing is the struggling, gutsy end of the business. You have to work the dickens out of your people and you can't pay them much because survival depends on keeping your over-head low. Our mission has always been to serve the low- and fixed-income people of our communities, and I quickly recog-nized the creativity and industriousness of our clientele. Why couldn't we recruit employees from that great base of talent?

They would be great at understanding and serving our customers because they *are* our customers. They could be excited about sharing the business with us. Couldn't we control overhead, give value to the customer, and still reward the employees?

The dog-eat-dog lens my father and grandfather had looked through would have to be replaced. Rather than overworking employees to control overhead, we would recruit people who could be motivated, to have an impact on others. The motivation to serve might pull creative and productive work out of all of us that would result in great overhead control and profound serving of *all* people. Retailing is a people business anyway, and if people are motivated, they actually work harder than if a boss yells at them to work hard. It's a different lens, a different approach.

I came to realize that this thing called authority only works when it's shared with everybody. That is key to the concept of followership. A real leader tries to vest his or her job in everybody else, in hopes of getting the best collectively actionable answers possible. The leader's own answer is somewhat irrelevant until the persons who must implement it also *own* it as *theirs!* And it's about knowing that you as leader don't *have* all the answers, so early on I admitted to those around me that I needed their help.

I never considered myself to be in authority over others so much as under the authority of others, and there is a quite a distinction there. In the Dollar General culture, authority has never been something you carry around as you bark orders to fearful subordinates. Rather, we hoped that every person we put into authority would feel the same sense of stewardship and responsibility I felt as the boss's son.

FROM THE DESK OF

J. Howard Olds

In my business, I answer to bishops, and in my years as a pastor I've seen all kinds. Some have been close friends. Most have had my admiration. Still, in all honesty, I would have to say that humility is not a virtue that often goes with the territory. You see, the very process of becoming a bishop in The United Methodist Church strokes the ego and feeds the sin of pride. The election process invites politics. The consecration service sets bishops apart. I have seen friends and colleagues go through dramatic personality changes in the process, taking on the authority of the office as a mandate to power and prestige.

There is one, though, who truly embodies the principles of followership. He manifests the qualities of being teachable, trustworthy, truthful, tenacious, and a team player. He stands out as a leader who humbly follows something greater than himself.

Bob Spain came to the Kentucky Conference in 1988 as a newly elected bishop with only four years to serve before retirement. Whatever he wanted to accomplish, he had to accomplish quickly. For some, that would be a ready excuse for strong-arm leadership, but that wasn't Bob. The first time I heard him speak, I was moved by his humility and obvious devotion to the Lord. He spoke of God as a friend, not as a theological proposition. He concluded his first annual conference by inviting pastors and lay people to pray at a makeshift altar before returning to their assignments. I had not seen this kind of humility from a bishop before. My first impression was that Bob Spain had avoided the pitfalls that trapped so many. He was still willing to learn from others and to walk humbly with his God. I was moved by that style of leadership.

During my four years of service under Bob, I dealt with him several times concerning my pastoral appointments, among other matters. At ordination, United Methodist pastors take the vow of itineracy, a commitment to go where sent by the bishop after due consultation. When your job and family are on the line, you appreciate a bishop who is truthful and trustworthy, and I found Bob Spain to be both. We were never bosom buddies. He kept his respectable distance, as good leaders should and do; but when it came to making my appointments, he exhibited personality traits I came to respect and admire. He was not insulted by my suggestions of places I would like to serve. He was not demanding when I hesitated over projected appointments. He was always willing to listen, even when I called him late at night to share my fear and anxiety.

We did not always agree. I particularly remember locking horns with him over the appointment of a person to the Conference Office. I was chair of the personnel committee, and we had our person. Bob and the cabinet had other people in mind. We debated over how to interpret our denomination's *Book of Discipline*. I protested for several hours. Finally, we agreed to disagree. The cabinet would make the appointment without the blessing of the personnel committee. When we met a few days later to announce and approve the decision, I asked Bishop Spain if he was angry about my protest. He put his arm around me and said, "Why should I be? You were doing what you thought was right." I like leaders with that kind of attitude. He stood his ground, but was willing to let me stand my ground as well. He did not need to use the authority of his office to whip me into line. I have not found all bishops to be that open and flexible while tenaciously holding their own positions.

Bob Spain was a team player, and that got him into trouble with people who interpreted the *Discipline* in strict legalistic terms. He was more interested in the spirit of the law than in the letter of the law. I watched ministers challenge him on the annual conference floor. They wanted Church law enforced. He wanted to do what was best for a person. It seemed to me that these kinds of conflicts eventually dampened his spirit and damaged his dreams for the Church. At heart he was a pastor, not a bishop, and when he had to decide between the two, his pastoral heart prevailed. Some would argue against that kind of leadership, but I found it to be refreshing. He often planted dreams that he knew would not become reality in his short tenure, but some of them did bear fruit after his departure.

In these latter days, it has been my privilege to become Bob Spain's pastor. I serve the church he once served and now attends regularly. It cannot be easy for any pastor, much less a bishop, to watch another minister lead the church he loves, and yet Bob Spain handles this situation graciously. These years have allowed a closer relationship than we had experienced previously. I find him still to be truthful and trustworthy, able to handle with sensitivity some of my deepest struggles. Even now, he is a team player. As his pastor, I observe his deep, abiding faith and benefit from his faithful, fruitful prayer life. And I have come to believe that his secret to leadership is simply this: First, foremost and forever, he is dedicated to following the Lord.

No one of us is perfect. We are not always what we long to be, but we can still strive to be single-minded, truehearted, and spiritually devoted. Leaders like Bob Spain, who truly follow the path God and life lay out for them, have the open-mindedness, the personal security, and the team-spiritedness to lead without pride. Such a spirit of leadership inspires others to develop their own potential and creates an organization that will have great impact on its industry and community.

QUESTIONS FOR REFLECTION

1. What do you think when you hear the word *follower*?

2. Can you think of a boss you've had in the past who was not a real leader? What distinguished that person from other leaders and mentors you've known?

3. What failures of leadership do you see in current events right now? What could those individuals have followed that would have helped them maintain their integrity in leadership?

CHAPTER 2

FOLLOWING THE PERSON INSIDE

You created my inmost being;
you knit me together in my mother's womb.
I praise you because I am fearfully and wonderfully made.

Psalm 139:13-14 (NIV)

The hit movie and Broadway musical *The Lion King* challenges us to think about the circle of life even as it entertains us in true Disney style. It is a tale of self-discovery about a young lion cub named Simba who is consecrated at birth to succeed his father, King Mufasa, as ruler of the Pridelands. Simba is born for leadership but nearly allows guilt and shame, induced by his jealous and evil-spirited uncle Scar, to destroy him.

Scar preys on Simba's youthful curiosity, luring him into the path of a wildebeest stampede in which Mufasa is killed trying to save his son. Scar convinces Simba that he is responsible for his father's death and urges him to run away from the Pridelands and never to return. Simba buys the lie and flees into exile, where he is befriended by a wacky warthog and a free-wheeling meerkat who teach Simba the Hakuna Matata ("no worries") attitude toward life. Still, something keeps him from being completely happy eating bugs and living as though nothing matters. He lives with great remorse and inner conflict about his past. Simba reaches a crisis point when he encounters his childhood friend Nala years later and learns of the suffering in the Pridelands under Scar's rule. Nala begs Simba to reclaim his role as king, but he is reluctant to return to the location of his childhood pain. Simba gains the courage to lead only when he hears the voice of his father thundering from the heavens, saying, "Simba, remember who you are." It is the acceptance of his unique identity that enables Simba to let the past go and return to his rightful place as king.

Who can resist being captured by a story like *The Lion King*? It is a little bit of *Hamlet*, the prodigal son, and everybody's autobiography rolled into one. Simba's growing awareness of himself and his place, and his resistance in facing his true calling, reflects a theme that has echoed through the sacred and secular literature of the ages. In fact, Simba in his hesitation has nothing on another potential leader reluctant to heed the call. That leader was Moses, and his story is one of the earliest and most compelling of all.

Moses' first words to God, in one of the Bible's most dramatic confrontations, were, "Who am I?" In the moment he first heard the voice in a bush burning on a mountaintop, Moses recognized the call of God, but he also recognized his own limitations, and he spoke out of pure fear.

"Who am I" he asked, "that I should go unto Pharaoh, and that I should bring forth the children of Israel out of Egypt?"

Moses spent that first conversation with God offering excuses, explaining why he was not the man for the mission. Finally, after each of his objections had been countered, Moses threw up his hands and asked God—unsuccessfully, as it turned out—to find someone else to run his errand.

It's hard to believe that this was the man of whom it was said, "Never since has there arisen a prophet in Israel like Moses, whom the LORD knew face to face. He was unequaled for all the signs and wonders that the LORD sent him to perform in the land of Egypt, against Pharaoh and all his servants and his entire land" (Deuteronomy 34:10-11). Moses would grow to become the quintessence of followership, a man who knew his calling, knew his people, and put the two together in a way that continues to ring true down through the ages. At the time, though, Moses had not yet seen himself the way God had always seen him. He didn't know what he could become if he were simply to live up to his potential.

Moses' journey provides us with a valuable lesson. Once we ask the question "Who am I?" we are led to the follow-up—"*Who might I be in light of the tasks laid before me? Whom can I grow to become?*" It was up to Moses to find the willingness to take on the challenges ahead. It is up to each of us to undertake the same process; for sooner or later, every man or woman, boy or girl must take the journey of self-discovery that reveals his or her true identity. And it is only as we discover honestly who we are that we are able to begin to lead in the essence of followership.

A LIFELONG SEARCH

The human journey begins inauspiciously and, in one sense, improbably enough. We start out as the seemingly chance meeting of sperm and egg, one of millions of possible combinations—and that's after father and mother have gone to the trouble of meeting! And yet out of all those possible embryos, all those potentially different human beings, we arrive on the planet with God's hand in the process and a unique purpose awaiting each of us. From that moment on, we are on a quest to discover the beauty and potential of our unique identities.

Children who are conceived in love and nurtured in healthy homes by parents who want the best for them arguably have a head start on this quest. If those of us from healthy, stable homes have trouble undertaking the quest for identity, how much tougher is it for those in difficult family situations? So many of us are born not knowing one or both parents. Others have parents troubled by personality disorders, substance abuse problems, and other handicaps. Scar may haunt us in the form of an uncle, an aunt, a parent, a sibling, a neighbor, or even a stranger who intentionally or unintentionally does us harm. Scar can also take the form of a voice inside us insisting we are guilty, unworthy, unloved, incapable.

Henri Nouwen once observed that we are born with "clenched fists." Maybe we instinctively know that we have both fears and fights ahead of us. Most of us manage to survive those helpless early years, of course. Parents get better with practice, and surroundings become more familiar with time. We even come to like the undivided attention and unlimited power we seem to possess with a simple cry or smile. These early experiences, our first interactions with our parents and a gradually widening circle of family and friends, do not survive as memories, but they do endure as some of the building blocks of our personalities.

We barely settle into this brave new world, getting used to doing things at our own pace, before all kinds of people begin to develop expectations of us. They want us to sleep when they say sleep, play when they say play, and develop some self-control over our tears and some restraint at the dinner table, especially if guests are present. Most of all, they want us to develop bladder and bowel control—our first good-bye to total freedom. Life does have its responsibilities!

Responsibilities quickly evolve into roles that we wrestle with and sometimes fight against for a lifetime. We are children, sons or daughters, citizens of certain ethnic origins, and participants in particular religious traditions or in none. We become students, employees, husbands or wives, parents, grandparents, doctors, lawyers, laborers, teachers, ministers, co-workers, or even CEOs. Some roles are more predictable than others. Some fit better and feel better than others. Herein lies our greatest dilemma beyond survival—the struggle between soul and role. In so many ways we are tempted to become what we do. We allow our identities as human beings to be shaped by the thoughts, statements, and expectations of significant others.

At some point in all this, if we are fortunate, we will begin to look for the person underneath all of the thoughts, fears, games, and roles that have piled up around us through the years. Whether we begin this quest in the face of a pressing mission, or whether the process begins with a small voice within or a big voice from on high, the moment we utter the simple question "Who am I?" we have done something profound—we have stepped onto holy ground, and seeking honestly to answer this question is a noble undertaking.

Some of the process involves getting a feel for the past, looking honestly at the present, and seeing the possibilities inherent in the future. It involves viewing our natural abilities in light of the outlooks and attitudes molded by our earliest experiences, by our encounters with family and friends, and then, as we grow, by our willful reactions to the world around us. We look at what we have been taught and what we have observed. We examine how all of that is manifesting itself in the here and now, and how it might serve us in the future—both the future we want and the one we actually get. If that seems like a tall order, keep in mind that, roughly, that is how we pick careers, spouses, friends, hobbies, and more.

"Who am I?" is a question for which we may never arrive at a complete answer, and yet asking it can be as empowering as it can be unsettling. We will never fully understand ourselves, because to question who we are is to grow and thus to redefine ourselves. The quest for self-awareness changes us even as we undertake it. Ideally, we strive to become better than the person we discover, forming a partnership with God to set the mark ever higher. In that way, self-discovery becomes a lifelong journey, one that meets and reacts to each new challenge, each new bit of awareness. We are all called to know ourselves, and in the process we will change into the person we need to be, or—if we let fear or selfishness or other negative emotions steer us in the wrong direction—into a sad reflection of what we might have been.

So many people today are experiencing deep crises of being. They have accomplished the right things, associated with the right people, pursued respectable careers, and yet have found themselves miserable. Somewhere in the midst of raising families, advancing professionally, and establishing themselves in communities, they lost their souls or, more likely, never took the time to find their souls in the first place. That's why the first challenge of adult life is to find ourselves—our true selves, the people we are inside. Some people manage to make this journey during late adolescence and early adulthood. They seem to have a naturally strong sense of their

God-given identity. The image of God (*Imago Dei*) that resides in their souls is healthy and whole.

The majority of us, however, have to search for the soul while dodging minefields of our own making. That's why midlife passages are so often midlife crises. The road to the soul is indented with all kinds of dead ends. Destructive habits, designed to compensate for a struggling soul, are hard to break, for breaking them leaves one feeling anxious and out of control. In addition, there is often a Scar hanging around in the shadows, with evil on his mind.

THE SIDE EFFECTS OF SELF-AWARENESS

Looking deep within for the person God created us to be does not always lead to confidence. Leaders, even great leaders, at times have doubts about themselves. Simba faced planted guilt at his supposed responsibility for his father's death. Moses doubted he had what it took for the immensity of the task of leading the Israelites out of bondage and into the Promised Land.

We are all insecure in some ways. We may mask it with bravado or arrogance, but most of us are smart enough to know that those relying most on bluff and bluster are those with the biggest insecurities. Those fears and insecurities may be exactly why we see so few real leaders among us. Many of us are reluctant to follow our true selves because that aspect of followership carries a formidable—some would say fearful—responsibility. Self-knowledge is not always pretty, and that fact derails many of us. We see the imperfections in our souls, and we think we are unworthy to lead. Along with Moses and other reluctant prophets, the Apostle Paul was highly conscious of his own shortcomings. Fortunately, he was able to rise above them as he ministered tirelessly throughout the Mediterranean. He was constantly returning to the source of his strength, the source of his very being.

All soul-searchers need to return to this Source. We are God-made.

"God breathed into the nostrils of humans the breath of life, and they became liv-ing beings" (Genesis 2:7 author's translation). That is more than poetry or a religious proposition. That is the truth of life and the single most im-portant fact about each of us. God made us and God loves us.

Henri Nouwen speaks to this when he says:

> We are the Beloved. We are intimately loved long before our parents, teachers, spouses, children and friends loved or wounded us. That's the truth of our lives. That's the truth I want you to claim for yourself. That's the truth spoken by the voice that says, "You are my Beloved."
>
> Listening to that voice with great inner attentiveness, I hear at my center words that say: "I have called you by name, from the very begin-ning. You are mine and I am yours. You are my Beloved, on you my favor rests. I have molded you in the depths of the earth and knitted you to-gether in your mother's womb. I have carved you in the palms of my hands and hidden you in the shadow of my embrace. I look at you with infinite tenderness and care for you with a care more intimate than that of a mother for her child. I have counted every hair on your head and guided you at every step. Wherever you go, I go with you, and wherever you rest, I keep watch . . . wherever you are I will be. Nothing will ever separate us. We are one."[1]

Simba was made in the image of his father. That was what the voice from the heavens told him. That is what he had to discover in order to be-come the leader he was born to be. And we are, each of us, created in the image of God. Those of us who profess Christianity know that explicitly, but often the journey of self-awareness is the process of re-discovering that staggeringly simple yet staggeringly profound fact. Each of us is a unique re-flection of that divine image and each of us is called to express it in some way. We must overcome our reluctance and embrace this fact. That is the story of every human being called to leadership.

There are complications awaiting us. We are special and yet we are weak. We reflect the divine and we reflect our humanity. Realizing both can put us at cross-purposes with ourselves. We protest in the presence of the spirit in the burning bush, and too many of us beg off from what we are called to do.

So we must remember, always, that before we are wounded by damaging words, tricked by evil intenders, dulled by daily demands, and driven by outside expectations; before we become the products of our own ambitions and fears, we are the children of God. Each of us has a God-given heritage on earth, the acknowledgment of which can be profoundly empowering. We are made to thrive, not merely survive.

Each of us is one of a kind, with unique spiritual and physical DNA; and while our stories may have similarities, each is as individual as we are. These stories follow us all the days of our lives or, more accurately, we follow them for a lifetime. Knowledge of our unique reflection of the image of God is too wonderful for us to comprehend fully, yet that is no cause for arrogance. It is a reason for deep gratitude and enduring responsibility.

Life does not require perfection of us—only awareness, since the more we understand our inner selves, the less likely we are to be blindsided by them. Even our limitations and hesitations can be redeemed to usefulness if they are brought to light, for the launching pad of leadership is self-knowledge. If we are to lead others effectively, we must follow the self we were created to be. Followership demands that we know who we are and that we lead from that centered awareness.

We do not gain these virtues overnight. In fact, we are always in process. But we can learn and grow and develop and become the persons God created us to be. We are uniquely and wonderfully made. When we decide to follow the person inside, we take a giant stride toward authentic personhood, which is the first prerequisite to authentic followership. Mufasa is right. "Remember who you are!" Then follow that true self.

FROM THE DESK OF

J. Howard Olds

I was raised in a religious family. My parents were small family farmers who made a decent living for their four children and gained the respect of the entire community. They taught us to work hard and worship God. They strictly enforced the Ten Commandments in our home. They required us to attend church services three times a week, and they taught us that honesty was the best policy. I am deeply grateful for this family foundation. Sometimes I stand amazed at the thought of my parents' accomplishments, given their humble beginnings. Thanks to them, I avoided most pitfalls of adolescence and gained a moral grounding that continues to guide me well. And yet my childhood was not without its struggles.

I was the youngest in that rural Kentucky family, seven years younger than my next sibling, my only brother. While my parents were upright and religious, they were not especially loving or affectionate. It was difficult, if not downright impossible, to gain their approval, however hard I might try. I cannot remember the words "I love you" ever being spoken inside my childhood home. My mother was deeply intuitive and intensely spiritual—and just as rigid as could be. Being the baby of the family, I was always in the way of the adults. I wanted to work in the fields, but I was too little. I wanted to play ball on Sunday afternoon, but I was a liability to the team. I wanted to sing in the church choir, but I was not big enough. I was teased a lot by other relatives and bullied continually by my older brother.

Parents don't like to admit they have favorites, but they do. Isaac loved Esau. Rachel loved Jacob. Joseph was obviously the chosen one over his twelve brothers—no wonder they sold him off to slavery in Egypt. Very early in my life, I set out to earn the blessing and approval of my parents, especially my father. I never got it from either of them. I excelled in school to earn the recognition that I missed at home. It definitely benefited my education, but it did nothing for my family standing. I gravitated to leadership positions, becoming the president of my high school class and holding multiple offices in school clubs and associations. I was named high school Citizen of the Year, but none of this changed my standing at home as the kid who always seemed to be in the way of others. Finally, I played the trump card. I announced I was going to college to study for the ministry. No one else in our family had attended college. Clergy, from my observation, were held in high esteem by my parents. Surely this would alter the tides of time. My father responded, "Well, you might as well be a preacher. You're too lazy to do anything else."

For years as an adult I pursued leadership positions in a desperate attempt to gain the recognition and approval of my parents or any other parental figures I could find. This "chasing after the wind" proved to be costly to my emotional maturity, my marriage, my colleagues, and, most of all, the congregations I was called to serve. I remember a pastoral counselor telling me a long time ago that I was the most ambitious person he had ever met and he didn't know how I would ever learn to handle it. It was about that time that I discovered Henri Nouwen's words quoted in this chapter. When it hit me that I was a loved child of God without proving anything, I cried for hours. That simple truth altered my whole approach to life.

I came to understand and love my parents before they died. Fortunately, my wife and children are patient and forgiving. I have learned the hard way that life is a matter not of competition but of cooperation with our innermost being. Finding my soul beneath all the roles I'd been playing brought me a deep sense of assurance and helped me redefine those roles and bring my true self to them. That is why following the person inside—the Image of God in each of us—is a key to fruitfulness and an answer to restlessness.

FROM THE DESK OF

CAL TURNER JR.

For all practical purposes, Dollar General and I were a joint founding. I was born three months after my father and grandfather founded J. L. Turner and Son Wholesale Notions and Hosiery; and given the realities of human physiology, I have to believe we were conceived at about the same time.

There were other similarities. I was the second of four "happy accidents," as my mother said of her children, and the company's entry into retailing was its second accidental milestone. The company got started in the first place because my dad and grandfather came across a big brick building for sale at half price, and a Turner would buy *anything* at half price. Then, the retail venture got started because my dad got stuck in ladies' panties.

Less than a decade after founding Turner and Son, with the economy in a post–World War II boom, my father had found a great bargain on a big lot of ladies' panties, and he took them to the small-town merchants he dealt with throughout Kentucky and Tennessee. These merchants, a conservative lot, said they weren't going to buy any more until they sold the last batch of panties he'd sold them.

"But these are even cheaper!" he told them. "Lower your prices and you'll sell more of them!"

They didn't buy his argument or his panties. They were trapped in the old economy, and he was trapped in ladies' undergarments. He had overbought, and if he couldn't move his panties through those other retail stores, then it was time for him and his father to open their own, where they could complement his aggressive buying with some smart selling.

The family business permeated the world around me as I grew up. My father and grandfather talked business as we waited in the living room for my grandma to finish preparing Sunday dinner. I would go with my dad on trips to visit stores. His driving always scared the heck out of me, so I would welcome the sight of one of our stores when we finally got there. Even my summer vacations were affected. In retailing, the back-to-school talk starts in the middle of the summer, so it would get underway just as I was enjoying my vacation from school, and I got to hating the retail business.

The Turner children also had interesting prayer lives. We were under our mother's mandate: "Pray for snow because your dad is overstocked on four-buckle overshoes and if he can't sell them, he can't pay off the banks—you need to pray every night until you get results." Just when we'd get that one accomplished, she'd hit us with the flip side: "It's almost Christmas, and customers can't get out to the stores with all the snow, so I want you to pray for the snow to melt."

Despite being immersed in the family business, my first career thought wasn't about retailing. It was about the ministry. I had had an overpowering and life-changing experience of Jesus Christ on a Sunday evening at the age of eleven. It came by way of music—the tune and the words to "The Old Rugged Cross" really got through to me and gave me a unique grounding in the sacrifice of Jesus. I knew right then and there how profoundly I was being affected, and I knew that my life would always be different from that time on—yet I still wondered what that difference would mean. I was terrified I might be called into the ministry, and that thought stayed with me for a long time. I had the chance to talk about it when I came home from Vanderbilt University after my sophomore year. Our Methodist church traded out pastors every four years or so, and when our new one, Brother Woodson, met me, he said, "Cal Jr., I understand you're considering the ministry."

"Yes, sir, I am," I told him.

"Well, I have some advice for you. Don't do it! Do something else. Do *anything* else, because only if there's nothing else you *can* do are you truly called into the ministry. There are far too many in ministry today who were never truly called in the first place."

That jolted me into serious thought about ministry, and I real-

ized that I did not really want to be a preacher. I didn't need little old ladies swooning over me and people pretending to listen
to my sermons every Sunday, and all the church politics and bureaucracy. It didn't feel right to me. But I was faced then with the
question—What is God calling me to do? The nagging thought
was that I was being called toward the family business, but that
scared me even more than the ministry had. I knew that my father would eventually run the business into the ground because
he would never turn it over to anyone but me, but I truly feared
losing my identity if I were to take on the role of boss's son.

I thought about my clerking experience as a teenager in the
Allen Dry Goods store on the square in Scottsville, Kentucky. I
wasn't any good at store work—to this day, I can't find anything—and so I got the customers nobody else wanted. I remember trying to make a sale to this old, weathered farmer
struggling over buying a 39-cent pair of panties (here we are
with panties again!) for his wife.

I asked him what size she wore, but he didn't know. I told him,
"Well, we have to know the size. How big is she?" He pointed to
my Aunt Ethel, who worked in the store. "She's about her size,"
he said. Now, I thought, we were getting somewhere.

Aunt Ethel was our best clerk, and at the moment she was
waiting on a customer. She had a big armful of merchandise she
was about to ring up.

"Ethel!" I yelled, in a voice that boomed across the crowded
store. "What size panties do you wear?" Well, she made a noise
like a gobbling turkey, threw the merchandise on the counter,
and went running, red-faced, to the stock room. I had thought it
was a very practical inquiry, just the thing to clinch my little bitty
39-cent sale; but given that we weren't going to get her cooperation, we just held the panties up and he tried to imagine
whether or not they'd fit.

As we talked, it occurred to me what vastly different lives we
led. The Turners weren't rich then, but I knew we were much better off than this poor old farmer, who was, like many of our customers, surely struggling just to get by. If there was anybody in
that community who needed help, it was he and those like him.

I thought, "Can't there be some positive influence I can have on the lives of people like that?"

I came to realize that maybe I could have much more effect on the lives of these people 24/7 through the business than I ever could by preaching sermons and listening to folks when they're troubled. I knew I would need to look at the everyday dynamics of the business differently if I was going to be called into it. I would have to look at retailing as a ministry.

I had thought that I hadn't been any good at all in my early retail experience, but my experience with that old farmer gave me a new outlook on retailing. I was wrestling with the call to ministry that had begun with my conversion experience, and ended up finding a calling that was, for me, much bigger and more fitting.

I chose my life's greatest challenge, which was to accept the subservience of ego necessary to go into business as the boss's son. It was the start of a lifetime in the family business, a lifetime, I hope, of serving others. The business became my ministry to a world full of hurt, pain, error, and sin—a ministry that, in my mind, is an even higher calling than the institutional ministry. It turns out I was called into ministry—it just wasn't in the way I expected.

QUESTIONS FOR REFLECTION

1. How did your upbringing help shape the person you are today?

2. Have you ever experienced an "identity crisis" or a time of struggling to "find yourself"? How did you come to know and accept the person God created you to be?

3. What aspects of your identity and calling could you follow in order to become a better leader?

CHAPTER 3

FOLLOWING THE PURPOSE OUTSIDE

"For I know the plans I have for you," declares the LORD, *"plans to prosper you and not to harm you, plans to give you hope and a future."*
Jeremiah 29:11 (NIV)

Renowned preacher Fred Craddock was once the dinner guest of some people who had adopted a greyhound when its racing days were fin-ished. He swears the following conversation took place, and since he was the only human in the room, who is there to question it? As the hosts pre-pared dinner, Fred and the dog wound up in the living room alone. Crad-dock glanced over at the aging greyhound and said, "So, you're retired?" The old dog lifted his head and replied, "Is that what they told you—that I retired?"

"They don't know the whole story," snorted the dog. "It happened like this. For years I raced around that track, my mouth watering for just a taste of that rabbit dangling on the stick in front of us. Year by year I got closer to the prize. Several times I came in second, passed at the finish line by an-other dog. It got so I could taste that rabbit in my sleep. It became my sole desire, to win a race. Then one day, I gave it all I had and even found the strength to make an extra charge at the end. It was enough. I won the race. I got the rabbit. Then I discovered it was a fake! They might have told you I retired, but I didn't retire—I quit! Who wants to spend the rest of his life chasing a fake rabbit?"

If we manage to address the identity question we dealt with in the last chapter, another comes barking at our heels. It is the mission question. Why am I here? What is my purpose? How does one spell success? How are God's plans for us revealed? If there is a will of God, how do I discern it? Every insightful person and effective organization must identify a clear mission and find the courage to follow it. Without such a mission, we will spend our lives running after fake rabbits.

Rick Warren, pastor of Saddleback Community Church in California, took the world by storm a few years ago with a best seller entitled *The Purpose Driven Life*. What was in this book that struck a nerve with millions of people around the world? Could the key be the fact that this book of faith straightforwardly states that our mission in life is not to make money, climb the corporate ladder, live in a selective neighborhood, get ahead, retire early, or even raise a fine family, as worthy as that may be? Life is not about you. It is not about me. What a revolutionary idea in a materialistic, self-centered, self-possessed society! As Warren so eloquently states, the purpose of life is to glorify God and enjoy God forever. Our mission in life is not to be served, but to serve. This isn't a new idea, of course; Jesus said that in the first century, to the chagrin of James and John, who were hoping for a promotion among the disciples. Paul suggested the same thing in his letters to the Romans, the Corinthians, and the Ephesians. Could this renewed awareness of ancient ideas about the purpose of life bring a significant shift in the goals and strategies of companies, communities, and churches? What if people really are tired of chasing fake rabbits?

Purpose-filled people are those who find their purpose outside by following the person inside. We saw in the last chapter that the self we uncover is a unique reflection of the God who created us. In finding our true selves we find the image of God, and it is in that place that we realize our true nature and our true calling.

"I know the plans I have for you," says the Lord to Jeremiah, and God has plans for all the rest of us. Most of us are not called into active institutional ministry. We are called instead, whether we acknowledge it or not, to bring a sense of ministry to bear on our families and careers, which provide the framework within which we conduct our lives and live out our beliefs. The goal of life is not climbing the corporate or ecclesial ladder. The truth is that we have a larger purpose, which may or may not include a specific career ladder but which is always in keeping with the person God created and planned for us to be.

DISCOVERING THE PURPOSE OF THE PERSON INSIDE

We will look first at the personal attributes that help us uncover the mission God holds in store for us. Then we will look at how we live out that mission in the day-to-day world we inhabit, whether we are in business or ministry, and how we can leverage our mission for greater leadership.

Each of us brings to the search for mission our own combination of traits and circumstances. Discovering this mission involves following the P.E.R.S.O.N. inside:

Personality

Experience

Reason

Spiritual Gifts

Opportunity

Need Awareness

These elements of our personhood describe not just our qualities and talents, but a unique blend of variables that offer insight into God's purpose for our lives.

All of us bring to work, to family, to life, certain **personality** traits. Some of us are extroverts while others are introverts. Some operate by intuition while others are more analytical. Some prefer to work alone. Others work best in groups. Surely it is the will of God for us to work from the sweet spots of our personalities, and yet businesses and churches do not always place people according to their personality strengths. Conversely, we aren't always careful about choosing jobs or careers that best match our dispositions. Forcing round personalities into square responsibilities is a sure way to court failure.

There is no substitute for **experience**. That is why field education and internships have become so critical in many schools. As valuable as education and natural aptitude are, it is not until we practice a certain job or task that we really know how suitable we are for that position, or how enjoyable we will find it. On-the-job training improves our skills. It also reveals our strengths and weaknesses. If we are given the right opportunities for feedback and reflection, experience can tell us a lot about our purpose in life.

Reason taps into God's wise plan for our lives. Where did we get the idea that God would have us do something for which we are entirely unsuited? Isaiah says the Lord wants us to reason together, and reason will help us weigh the many options for using our time and energy.

Tony Campolo likes to tell the story of hearing a teenager he met at a housing project basketball court say that he planned to become an NBA basketball star and make millions of dollars. "What makes you think you can do that?" asked Campolo. "My teacher told us we could be anything we wanted to be," said the kid. The seventy-year-old Campolo challenged the seventeen-year-old kid to a one-on-one game and outscored him eleven baskets to one. It was a lesson in Reality 101: a dream unrooted in plausibility is wasted mental effort.

Spiritual gifts are God-given abilities to be used for the good of others. There are all kinds—teaching, preaching, leading, giving, encouraging, healing—the list goes on and on. Paul, who cites many of them in his letter to the Corinthians, compares them to different parts of the body, each one functioning for the good of the whole. This is what separates talents from spiritual gifts. Cooking, public speaking, or playing piano, for example, are just talents until they are used to benefit others.

Purpose is driven by **opportunity**. In many cases, the great leaders of the world did not set out to make names for themselves. They were not looking for a shot at stardom. They just did what needed to be done at the moment. In a 2007 sermon celebrating the life and legacy of Dr. Martin Luther King, Jr., James Lawson asserted that Dr. King never intended to become a civil rights leader. He never planned to be in Montgomery, Alabama, when Rosa Parks staged her now-famous sit-down in the front of the bus. He even declined the first call to lead the city boycott. Dr. King wanted to be the president of Morehouse College in Atlanta, and had just accepted the position at Dexter Avenue Baptist Church to wait for a position to open at the college. Obviously, God had another opportunity in mind for Martin Luther King, Jr.; and, fortunately for the world, Dr. King recognized it. We may discover our purpose simply by being open to the opportunities God puts before us.

We, like Dr. King, may make plans, but we should be ready to be redirected by the **need** at hand, which can define our purpose in life. To paraphrase Frederick Buechner, our God-given purpose is where our gifts meet the needs of the world. Purpose-driven people seek out opportunities to meet others' needs, and rise to the occasion when a need presents itself.

FROM VISION TO REALITY

Purpose-driven people have vision, a picture of the way things ought to be and, indeed, can be if the right elements come together at the right time in the right way. The vision of Dollar General is "a better life for everyone." The vision of Brentwood United Methodist Church is "touching hearts, transforming lives for the glory of God and the good of the world." Visions are neither self-centered nor self-serving. They are faith-based and hope-full. Visions can begin the process of reshaping the world.

The Bible is the most visionary book ever written. It is full of people pursuing God-given visions. God gave Abraham the vision of a new nation whose numbers would equal the sands of the sea. Moses led the children of Israel out of Egyptian bondage in pursuit of the envisioned promised land. Jesus had a vision that a handful of disciples empowered by the Holy Spirit could change the world. John the Evangelist had a vision that evil will be defeated, suffering will end, tears will be wiped away, and the Lord God Omnipotent will reign forever and ever. These were people empowered with extraordinary pictures of God's preferred future, and, most of all, the courage and faith to make those visions a reality.

What dreams of a better world dance in your mind? What thoughts of a better company, a better church, or a finer community capture you from time to time? Share your vision with other people. Test it over time. Persevere through the questions and oppositions. Let the vision grow beyond your control.

A vision, of course, is only a starting point. Without action, a vision is simply a daydream. To serve as a guide, it must be translated into a mission, which is a statement of a person or organization's role in attaining the vision.

On a divine scale, mission is our higher calling, the way we live out God's plan for us on earth. A life in business or even in the ministry is a subset of that grand calling, and it will have its own mission. The visions of our two organizations were mentioned above, but our mission statements are what help us embody those visions. For Dollar General to achieve its vision of "a better life for everyone," we must live out our mission to "serve others." It is the mission of Brentwood United Methodist Church to "make disciples of Jesus Christ"; and by doing that, we believe we can touch hearts and transform lives for the glory of God and the good of people. Good mission statements keep us focused. They help us remember that "the main thing is to keep the main thing the main thing."

We must beware, however, lest we make our mission on earth so narrow and selfish that we fulfill it too easily and lose our reason for living long before we die. That can happen when we confuse a goal, which is a task with a foreseeable end, and a mission, which is a much loftier, much grander concept.

Management expert Larry Appley clarifies the distinction with this story: A woman once stopped to watch two men pouring concrete on a hot summer day.

"What are you doing?" she said to one.

"I'm pouring concrete—can't you see?" he said.

The other looked up and said, "I'm laying the foundation for an office building that's going to be the pride and joy of the downtown area for generations."

One of those men had an objective. The other had a mission.

A mission is the motivating purpose that pulls the best out of an institution or business through its people. Mission is motivational, positive, perpetually challenging. Mission gives us a base for reacting to events, because it doesn't change in spite of what's going on around us. With a shared mission, people can sustain their enthusiasm because a mission is constantly prompting goals and inspiring strategies. And when a leader is in tune with the others, helping to bring mission to bear on action undertaken by people empowered for those tasks, you have the basis for the kind of teamwork true followership is designed to foster (as we will explore in depth in the next chapter). Such a leader will be able to inspire the best in others.

Far from being pie in the sky, mission has relevance to everyday living. It is the vehicle that carries us toward the promised land, which is the vision. As the story of the workers pouring concrete illustrates, two people can be doing the same task and look identical from the outside; but if one has an objective and the other is carrying out a mission, there will be a world of difference. One has an overview that carries him toward a future that's clear and compelling in his head. The other is simply slogging through life.

Each of us has God-given talents we're called to actualize. We have seen how our purpose lies in that place where our gifts meet the needs of the world. Following our purpose helps us recognize and pursue that place within ourselves and helps us actualize it in those around us, inspiring them toward a common mission. Without a genuine mission born of vision, work loses meaning. In that sense, mission is a very practical thing. Without it, it's possible for a group of people to get all fired up by a seminar, a speech, a retreat, or a boss's pep talk, and emerge truly euphoric but without a clue as to what's going on, without a real plan or a course of action for the future.

During World War II there was only one radio in Scottsville, Kentucky, and quite a few of the locals had gathered around it to listen to one of President Franklin Roosevelt's fireside chats. When it was over, people were discussing what a wonderful talk it was, and how good everyone felt. Finally, one of them said, "You heard him and I heard him, and it was a very nice speech. But—who's winning the war?" Visions provide the necessary inspiration, but people are likely to lose motivation without a clearly stated purpose and progress report.

The inspired leader is someone through whom the mission is brought to bear on the day-to-day activities of the people in an organization, bringing those activities into clear focus and putting them in context. Once we establish our personal and corporate mission statements, the process continues with goals and strategies, strategic objectives, operational objectives, and operational action plans. All of those grow out of the mission and get their focus from it. Even as the mission inspires us, it must enable us to focus on specific tasks in very practical ways and prompt action on them. Ultimately, the mission must be shared in such a way that it can be passed along faithfully and effectively throughout the organization for years into the future.

The leader who faithfully follows his or her purpose will want to share with others the process of self-discovery and of turning mission into action. He or she will model that dynamic for others in the organization so that what is passed along is a real legacy, the means for discovering and developing personal and institutional identity, enabling others to pick up where the leader left off. Consider the passing of the torch from Moses to Joshua. Moses never made it to the promised land. A brief moment of doubt in the form of two strikes of a rock with his staff cost him that opportunity, but those around him had seen the process in motion in him and were able to continue his work. In that sense, mission is intergenerational. It is what allows the histories of churches and corporations to unfold over the decades, and it is what has allowed the church to continue its work through the centuries.

Without a meaningful purpose, we are the greyhound chasing the fake rabbit, and no living creatures want to spend their lives chasing fake rabbits—not dogs and certainly not humans. If God really does have a plan for each life, then we are wise to discern that plan, pursue it, and turn it into a mission statement that guides our goals, our strategies, and our day-to-day lives. We will at times have to set course corrections, but the mission will remain a beacon on sometimes choppy seas. If we are faithful, we will act to the best of our abilities in concert with others for the glory of God and the good of all people. The process we follow includes insight into the persons we are, a vision of what might be, the statement of mission that embodies the vision, and strategic goals and plans to measure our success effectively. Following our purpose empowers us to live lives filled with real accomplishment and true meaning.

FROM THE DESK OF
CAL TURNER JR.

When I came into the top responsibility for the development of Dollar General in 1965, I found a company in entrepreneurial chaos. We had no defined purpose or plan. We didn't even have an organizational chart, and if we'd had one it would have required round paper, with my dad in the middle and a lot of spokes going to God-only-knows-where.

From 1968, when my dad put me in charge of the initial public offering of Dollar General, until 1977, when I became president, I winged it with Wall Street, which didn't know what to do with us. They didn't know how to assign a price/earnings multiple to a company they couldn't categorize. We weren't a discounter, we weren't a variety store, and we weren't a department store. We were a dollar store, which was a new concept at that time.

In 1977, I moved from boss's son to the leader responsible for the future of the company. I thought, "Oh my gosh, I've got to have some training," and I went away to take the American Management Association's management course for presidents. That's when I learned the importance of strategic planning, and I knew I had to convince Daddy of its importance as well. I thought, "I have to get the attention of the old mule, and sometimes the best way to do that is with a plank." So, I came home after the training, walked into Daddy's office, shut the door, and sat down to wait for him to get off the telephone. Turners do talk a lot, you know. When he did, I said, "Daddy, we have a decision to make."

"What's that, Son?"

"Our decision is whether to do strategic planning now or wait until you're dead!"

"What *is* strategic planning?"

I knew at that moment I had the attention of the mule.

So I told him, "This company operates as if there's a door that says 'Turner' on one side and it's closed to everybody else. Strategic planning is a process to open that door to the non-Turners to get their input and increase their ownership of this company. We need honest discussion with them about our strengths and weaknesses and opportunities and threats. Then we need their thoughtful suggestions about how the company should be changed. They'll be the ones implementing the change, so they will own it and they will be committed to doing it well."

He paused, and then said, "Well, Son, I know that the way I've always run the company is not the right way for it to be run in the future. I do not know what that right way is, but I do respect you and support your figuring that out. But remember—I don't want y'all to be '*plan planners*.' I want you to be '*plan doers*'!"

My father had an innate grasp of the downside of strategic planning, how it can take on a life of its own within organizations and become more about the planning itself than about implementation. The Turner approach he was advocating was halfway between the extremes of overplanning, which many people are prone to, and not planning at all. We sometimes referred to this middle way of planning as "planning on the run" because even good planning requires flexibility in the real world. We agreed to work on a strategic plan and put it into action to see how it worked, then tweak it as we went along. We saw our approach work in the next decade as the company took off. I took pride in the fact that strategic planning, which seldom occurs in operations-oriented retailing, did occur at Dollar General, resulting in a renewed excitement for the prospects of extreme-value retailing.

Our company had operated too long without a clearly stated vision for the future. One of the keys to our success was a clear—yet flexible—strategic plan that drew on the insights of everyone in the company. Following our purpose meant engaging in an ongoing process of corporate self-discovery. The best strategic planning is not academic. It is people-centered and dynamic.

FROM THE DESK OF

J. Howard Olds

Ministry is in my bones. My calling has been there, I think, since my birth. When I was eight years old, I used to play church. I would line up the kitchen chairs in our tiny little living room, put hymnals out, and get up in the front and preach. I've been known to tell the people in our pews on occasion, "Those empty chairs were about as responsive as you are now."

By the time I was twelve, I was wrestling with this notion that maybe I was being called to professional ministry. I saw the church as a place of comfort and safety, a place to run to when I didn't like it at home. I often felt that I didn't fit in at home. I felt that I was in the way, that I'd been abandoned. But I never felt abandoned by God. During my worst of times as an adolescent, God was a refuge. Since the beginning, I wanted to be a preacher, and that calling has never fundamentally altered.

I think part of the appeal might have been the student ministers who were coming into town, and by the time I was sixteen or seventeen I knew that was what I wanted to do with my life. I knew I belonged in a local church where I could preach and where I could hold people's hands at critical moments in their lives. I didn't even know what colleges were available, and I went to Asbury just because that's where the student pastors to our church came from.

I was eighteen when I took my first appointment to two little churches. One of them had about eight members, one of them sixteen. There would be from two to ten people in church on Sunday. I used to dream about the three big churches that I wanted to lead in Kentucky, but the guiding hand of God led me elsewhere, sometimes against my will. In the early years of the twenty-first century, a series of circumstances gave me the opportunity to use my gifts for ministry in a congregation in Brentwood, Tennessee. This church was not even on my radar screen. I had never dreamed about a church of this size or potential, but my time at Brentwood United Methodist Church has thus far capped a calling that I have truly loved and appreciated.

Just before that move, in 2000, I was nominated for the episcopacy, and my name was circulated across the denomination. Not long afterward, a man who had been a student pastor in our little church when I was five or six years old called me. He was in California, and I hadn't talked to him in years. He told me that he'd heard about my nomination for the episcopacy, and said, "I think there's something you need to know." He said that when I was no more than five, my mother was praying at the altar in that church. She looked up at him and said, "The Lord just told me that Bubby [as I was called then] is going to be a minister." She never mentioned that to me, even though I had been a pastor for fifteen years when she died. "I just thought maybe you need to know that," he said.

His fifty-year-old story confirmed to me that I had indeed been a minister since birth. I never did choose it. It's just always been there, and I think that's why I never burned out as other pastors have. I've gotten tired and weary, and I've had my moments with it along the way, but I bounced back and I love it now more than I ever have. Health problems and all, my passion is as alive at sixty-two as when I first preached to that empty row of chairs.

QUESTIONS FOR REFLECTION

1. What do your **P**ersonality, your **E**xperiences, **R**eason, your **S**piritual gifts, the **O**pportunities you face, and the **N**eeds in your community tell you about your purpose in life?

2. Describe your vision for the future of your organization, your family, or your community. What steps can you take to help make that vision a reality?

3. What is the mission statement of your church or company? Are there clear paths and plans laid out for you to follow in pursuit of that mission?

4. What is your purpose in life? If you don't already have a personal mission statement, consider writing one to inspire and guide you as you live out your purpose.

CHAPTER 4

FOLLOWING OTHERS

Leaders are more powerful role models when they learn than when they teach.

Rosabeth Moss Kantor

One of Sweden's most popular tourist attractions is a great oaken warship called the *Vasa*. Commissioned by King Gustavus Adolphus and named for his family, it was the most powerful vessel on earth when it was launched in 1628. To stand before it is to be swept back to a time when woodsmen felled huge stands of virgin timber for use in magnificent ships designed to be intimidating both militarily and psychologically. More than 220 feet long and 17 stories tall from keel to mast, the *Vasa* was to be the pride of the Swedish navy, a fearsome symbol of the king's power in the region. It had 64 cannons—each bearing the king's initials—and many ornately carved statues designed to terrify enemies.

As it turned out, though, the ship never terrified anyone. Just 20 minutes after embarking on its maiden voyage, before thousands of spectators in awe of their king's dominion, the great sailing vessel caught a stiff breeze, listed hard to port, took on water, and sank 100 yards from shore, to lie on the bottom until its salvage in 1961.

The straightforward explanation for why the ship sank was that it was top-heavy—it had too many heavy guns sitting too high on the hull. The deeper reason, though, is that the process that built the ship was just as top-heavy. The king, though no expert on shipbuilding, decreed some of the vessel's specifications. Legend has it that when he heard that his archrival, the Danish king, had commissioned a ship with two gun decks, the king ordered a second be added to the *Vasa* as well, although the ship had only been designed for one. He also insisted on a quick construction schedule that prompted a number of shortcuts. The king, who was considered infallible, was busy leading troops in Prussia, and no one had the authority to change the plans or the temerity to question his orders, even though some of them knew they could be heading toward disaster. No one dared to deal with the problems that arose. As a result, a massive expenditure of human labor—not to mention 4 percent of the country's budget—lay at the chilly harbor bottom for three-and-a-half centuries.

The *Vasa* is a monument to one of the great traps of leadership. Unfortunately, management disasters of this kind are not unique. If you're a student of business, government, or the military, you know of countless instances where the person at the top issued an order that was carried out faithfully—and disastrously. The *Vasa* illustrates how difficult it can be for a leader to be in touch with the truth. Even the people who love and respect a leader will shade or withhold the truth rather than risk the leader's displeasure. Oftentimes those subordinates even have subordinates of their own protecting *them*. It's possible for the leader of an enterprise to be one of the most ill-informed persons in it! The *Vasa* might seem to be an extreme example, but to one degree or another, such problems exist in every organization and in every situation involving leadership. It goes with the turf, and the more successful the leader, the more effort required to cut through the well-intentioned misinformation.

TOGETHER EVERYONE ACHIEVES MORE

One of history's great lessons is that leaders are fallible. Iron fist or velvet glove, one-person rule is fraught with peril. That's not to say there isn't a time for top-down, don't-ask-questions management. At the start of a battle, when the ball is teed up for the kickoff, when the building is burning, a strong, steady hand can be the only sensible choice. You want results, and the time for consultation is over. Most of the time, though, there is another, better way.

People have been conditioned to believe that success in church, in business, or in other organizations consists of finding the right driver. To borrow Jim Collins's metaphor in his bestseller *Good to Great*, let us tell you that getting the right people on the bus and assigning them the right seat is even more important.

There's no doubt that the right leader is crucial. A leader can serve as a focal point, an organizer, an inspirer, an anchor. People look for standard-bearers. But we've seen that a brilliant leader with a flawed program is no bargain. Neither is a talented CEO unable to see past his or her own pet ideas. Life has simply become too complicated for any one person to manage everything. This is why leaders must follow the wisdom and creativity of their team so that everyone is informed and empowered enough to facilitate the organization's success.

We have talked in the preceding chapters about the nature of followership and about the process of looking inside ourselves and finding a mission to pursue. Unlike the other concepts we follow, this chapter is about other *persons*, flesh-and-blood human beings reflecting God's image in their own way. That, of course, puts us on another plane entirely. Great leaders will respect and work to develop each person's God-given strengths, and have the humility and discernment to follow others' ideas and gifts when the situation calls for it.

Following others is about accomplishing results through and with others. It draws on the men and women of an organization, church, or business, and accomplishes together more than any of the individuals could achieve alone—most likely more than they think possible. But what kind of relationship does the true disciple of followership have with the others in a business, church, or organization? Julius Caesar was one of history's great military leaders. He was a brilliant tactician, but perhaps more important, he was great at getting the most out of his men, at inspiring superhuman effort in otherwise demoralized troops, soldiers who would not have done nearly as well under anyone else. He did it in part by fighting alongside them, sharing their hardships, and passing along many of the spoils of war to them. We can do the same by sharing credit, praising our teammates when they do well, and offering genuine encouragement when they struggle. It is the connection and relationship between the leader and the others in an organization that really matters.

COMMUNICATING CLEARLY AND HONESTLY

Good leadership is predicated on the flow of information from the top down and also from the bottom up. News has to spread as smoothly as possible in all directions within an organization; and when there is a problem, it should be solved quickly and by those closest to the problem. Therefore, the highest skill of leadership is communication. This entails not just listening to others and sharing ideas freely, but internalizing others' viewpoints and discussing them openly and honestly. Communication is key to nurturing the success of others sharing the mission.

It is also leadership's greatest challenge. Both the need for good, clear communication and impediments to it are ever-present. When it comes to communication and leaders, there are two kinds of impediments—external and internal. Externally, one of the chief offenders is a rigid, inflexible organization. Few things can stifle creativity or efficiency quite as effectively. Governmental entities are notorious for turning seemingly simple matters into hopeless bureaucratic tangles, and sadly, many churches mire their ministries in miles of red tape as well, bogging them down with boards and committees. Structure is, of course, essential. A CEO can't deal with every little matter in every little store. Chains of command help sift and organize information as it is passed upward, and apply it as it is passed down. Too often, though, lines of communication become blocked and streams of information hit logjams. One of the biggest challenges of communication is to ensure that an organization's culture and structures facilitate rather than hinder creativity and enthusiasm, which bureaucracy quite often stamps out.

Internally, the leader's image, body language, and style of communicating can do far more to discourage the free flow of information than a flawed organizational structure. Feelings of superiority and distrust of the motives of others within the organization can all be detrimental to the task at hand. Lack of respect for others and their contributions is deadly. True leaders believe deep in their souls that other people are important, while mere managers may not. A manager might say, "I'm in charge here. I will tell them what to do, and they had darn well better do it." That's not a leader. That's a manager with an outsized ego, too insecure to follow others to greater success for the whole organization.

A great definition of communication came from Larry Appley, the long-time chairman of the American Management Association. According to Appley, communication is "joint creativity based on mutual respect." Communication is a process that allows two individually creative persons to become even more creative together because of their grounding in mutual respect. That respect sparks a synergy wherein each inspires greater creativity in the other. The true leader sees communication as a tool with which to elicit from others the best that they have while imparting the best in return.

Appley identifies two critical traits that form the psychological underpinning of creative communication—intellectual maturity and emotional stability. Intellectual maturity, Appley maintained, involves having the grounding and convictions to take a stand in important matters and to do so in a timely way. Real leaders do not let a void remain when the time has come for a decision, though they are always aware that it is never possible to have all the facts. A leader also has to be mature enough to deal with new facts that may arise, to admit that an earlier decision was wrong, based on the discovery of new facts or insights, and to humbly make the warranted changes. Emotional stability requires living in step with one's convictions. All of us will have some gap between our ideals and our actions—we are, after all, human—but if the gap is too great, a person isn't stable enough to lead others. Great leaders work toward minimizing that gap.

A leader well grounded in both intellectual maturity and emotional stability has the foundational mindset upon which creative communication can be built, using certain techniques and strategies. Let us consider three major strategies of effective communication, using the disaster of Gustavus Adolphus and the *Vasa* as a case study.

The first, which underlies the success of all other communication strategies, is the most important and most often neglected step of all: **setting the climate**. Communication is best advanced where there is comfort, respect, and an even playing field. If one person feels off-balance, undervalued, or uncomfortable, his or her contribution to the team may be compromised. This step is taken in a variety of ways depending on the setting and subject of the discussion—the climate set for a Bible study would be different than for a locker room meeting or for a gathering of regional managers or stockholders. Each has its own important elements, but in every case, a group will take its cue from the leader, for better or for worse.

An "even playing field" would have been unthinkable in the Swedish royal court of the seventeenth century, but Gustavus Adolphus could have taken steps to help his subordinates feel more comfortable advising him against the design changes that led to the *Vasa's* sinking. He could have taken the time to listen to people experienced in shipbuilding, rather than spouting off his own demands. He could have visited the shipyard rather than sending cursory letters from abroad. In many ways, the *Vasa* was doomed from the start because the king was a pompous boss, not a true leader with respect for honest communication.

Once the climate is set, **two-way discussion** will ensure that both the problem and all possible solutions are presented clearly. Communication involves real give and take, where all team members feel free both to ask and answer questions because they know their input is valued. Following others means genuinely respecting and valuing colleagues' information, ideas, and unique perspectives because they are the people on the front lines who are privy to the day-to-day details of life in the trenches.

Leaders should first present the issue or problem at hand in a focused, organized manner, ensuring that everyone understands the nature and agenda of the meeting. In non-emergency situations, the true leader will simply present the problem or the issue without mandating a specific course of action, and then invite honest feedback from others on the team. Real listening requires hearing what isn't said as well as what is, and seeking to clarify both with probing questions designed to elicit the genius on the front lines. A leader can draw out this genius with the right questions and the right encouragement; and since the leader is in possession of a wider perspective, he or she can place it in context and make the best use of it. Meetings and strategy sessions aren't about the leader presenting a preordained solution for everyone to salute. The great leader will have the humility to recognize the need for broad input and to value the creative solutions offered. A good leader does not make quick value judgments on the answers received, or state his or her disagreement right away, since criticism will turn off the spigot of creativity. A good leader asks strategic questions and gathers the bad with the good, maintaining a climate conducive to honest revelation.

What if Gustavus Adolphus had valued two-way communication? He would have refrained from asserting his own opinions and desires, instead explaining the objective of having a better-equipped battleship. He might have presented his idea of giving the *Vasa* two gun decks instead of one, rather than mandating the decision against good counsel. He would have listened to the shipbuilders' explanation of how a second gun deck would make the ship top-heavy, and genuinely considered their alternative ideas for making the *Vasa* just as impressive and well-armed as the Danish ship with which the king wanted to compete. Since Gustavus Adolphus obviously did not understand much about a ship's center of gravity, probing questions about the engineering of the *Vasa* and the ideas the shipbuilders presented would have helped

Sweden as a nation improve its navy with a ship that was both impressively armed and stable enough to be seaworthy.

After setting a respectful climate and practicing two-way communication, it is important to **clarify the solution**. As questions are asked and answered, all parties should paraphrase what they hear the other saying. Paraphrasing—the prerequisite of a listening mindset—helps ensure that we are responding to the other person's actual statement, rather than to our own initial impression of what was said. It's the most efficient way to find out immediately if you have misunderstood, if the other person has misspoken, or if there is some other breakdown in communication. We cannot follow others' insights and contributions if we do not understand them. So it is crucial that all parties understand clearly what solution has been determined, whether this is communicated by the end of the meeting or at some point soon thereafter, if the leader has taken time to consider the matter independently after hearing the group's input. Clarifying the solution helps the team members to know that the leader has taken their contributions seriously.

Imagine once again the discussion between Gustavus Adolphus and the designers of the *Vasa*. Had the king set a climate of respectful communication and welcomed the suggestions of the shipbuilders, several ideas might have emerged for how to arm the ship in a way that would not have undermined its structural integrity. The king could have then paraphrased the suggested plan, verified that he understood the idea correctly, and responded appropriately. By using better communication strategies than his original despotic technique, Gustavus Adolphus could have followed the wisdom of his shipbuilders and clarified a solution with them that would have resulted in a ship worthy of and useful to the Swedish navy.

TRUE LEADERSHIP BENEFITS EVERYONE

The ultimate goal of communication is human development. Keeping this goal in mind results in leadership that fosters holistic growth and productivity all around, for individuals as well as for institutions. True leadership does not seek to make others into clones of the leader, or to define them solely in terms of the corporation, church, or organization. It seeks rather to foster and to celebrate the development of each person's unique talents. Following others is never about using them for personal or corporate gain. While it accomplishes a mission with and through them, it is a catalyst for their growth, for the maximum development of their potential. It shows the ultimate in regard for others.

What can we expect to gain from following others? In a church or business where people are valued and appreciated—where followership has transformed conventional leadership—the atmosphere is electric. People are glad to be there. They are eager to help. They are comfortable in their jobs and generally positive about life. When people are affirmed for what they do, they work harder. Their level of commitment rises. People own what they help to plan, and when they invest themselves in a project, they will feel a personal obligation to make it succeed. Where everyone is valued and where there is team ownership, there is a real sense of community. People feel that they belong. They care about each other. Communities double joys and halve sorrows.

Followership makes for the kinds of workplaces, churches, and organizations that attract people. Leaders who follow the contributions of those around them know that the ideas floating in such people's minds can be more helpful than all the books we could ever read, and that the energy and enthusiasm unleashed from within them can transform them and their organizations.

FROM THE DESK OF

J. Howard Olds

At age twenty-nine, I became Annie Laurie's pastor. She had retired after decades of teaching speech in a public high school, and she and her husband Russ were very active in that growing church. As I greeted attendees after leading my first worship service, several ventured guesses about my background based upon my accent. Most were sure I hailed from the Deep South. Annie Laurie overheard several of those conversations as she stood patiently in line to greet her new pastor. Finally, she interrupted my greeting of a worshiper to say, "That boy is not from the South. Only people from Owen County talk like that. He's less than fifty miles from home. I would recognize that accent anywhere." I could tell right away that I might have trouble getting along with this gruffly outspoken old woman.

My fears multiplied the next Sunday when she handed me her worship bulletin at the close of the service—on it, she had noted every grammatical error I had made during worship. She did it again the next Sunday and the Sunday after that, and I knew I was in for a long tenure. After I had been there awhile, however, I began to see the kindness behind the brash exterior. She took me aside and said, "People here really seem to love you." A little later she told me, "You're doing a great job." I gradually realized, "Hey! This person is on my side!" Those weekly bulletins noting my use of "was" when "were" would have been correct—and I would get them for the entire nine years I was at that church—were her way of using her knowledge to make me a better speaker. She had lovingly taken this twenty-nine-year-old preacher under her wing, and, thankfully, I was smart enough to realize I needed what she had. I had come out of a country farm community where nobody taught you proper etiquette or correct grammar, and there was a lot I was lacking. She had thought, *I'll take this country kid and polish him up a little bit.* She was a godsend. I came to admire and appreciate the very things I had detested and despised at first.

Annie Laurie became my best friend. When I wrote the dissertation for my doctoral degree, I gave the rough draft to Annie Laurie for grammatical correction. I even included several pages of nothing but punctuation marks with a note that said, "Please feel free to place these in the appropriate places." When she and her husband died, years after I'd gone on to another church, I came back and conducted their funerals. Annie Laurie left an indelible stamp on me, and although I never formally enrolled in one of her speech classes, she became one of my most cherished teachers.

FROM THE DESK OF
CAL TURNER JR.

Our relations with others are probably the best indicators of whether we've got a handle on leadership. I've watched as three generations of Turners have struggled to get it right, and I've learned a number of valuable lessons along the way.

From my grandfather, Luther Turner, I learned something about hard work and humility. Luther was eleven when his father was killed in a freak accident, the result of horseplay gone tragically wrong. With just three years of schooling behind him, Luther was forced to take over the family's Macon County, Tennessee, farm. The soil was poor, the farm was mortgaged, and he had three younger siblings to help feed and raise. But even at that age, J. L. Turner was a hard worker; and as he matured and got stronger, he earned a reputation as the hardest-working farmer in the area. So when the farmers decided to open a co-op store, even though he was the youngest among them, he was asked to manage it. It was the beginning of retailing for the Turners, and though the work was definitely hard, it was much easier than farming!

There were two things J. L. Turner carried from those tough early years into the successful years of his later life. First was the willingness to work hard. Second was the lifelong assumption that there was something he could learn from everyone he met, because chances are that person was better educated than he was. He was one of the smartest men I ever knew on a wide range of subjects because his agenda was to learn from others. He never thought he had all the answers.

I always held that up as a very valuable asset for everybody who worked at Dollar General. Carry the assumption that every single person you meet has something valuable to teach you. They may not even know what it is, but if you assume it's there, and if you set the right climate and ask the right questions, you will find it.

From my father—and a friend's father—I learned about the power of praise. The friend had a life track that ran parallel to mine. He too was a *junior*, and like me, he was a boss's son being groomed to take over the company. He was smarter, better looking, and better educated than I, but he never received his father's blessing. When he came home with all A's except one B, his father would come down hard on him. When I came home with all A's except one B, my dad would say, "Son, I never thought a Turner would earn grades this good—that is wonderful." It was just the way my father was. My first job was sweeping the floor in our warehouse after school, and Dad would make a point of walking with an associate down an aisle I'd just swept. He'd say, "Look at this. Have you ever seen a floor that was swept as well as this one?" as if he didn't know I was in the next aisle listening! He was always giving me approval. I grew up knowing what it meant to be praised for what I did and how important that can be.

And then there are the many lessons I've had to learn myself. One in particular reminded me that Luther was right, that there is something to learn from everyone, no matter which side of the classroom or leadership aisle he or she is on. I was speaking to senior executives at a leadership development training program, telling them about the importance of a personal mission statement. I told them that it should be brief and motivating, something you could never fully accomplish but which would help you screw your head on straight every day. I shared Dollar General's mission statement—Serving Others—and then, as I encouraged them to write their personal mission statement, I shared mine. At the time, it was, "Rejoicing in my God-given potential and developing it to the fullest in a way that encourages others to do the same." It was actually quite a mouthful, given what I had just said about brevity. When I'd finished, a slight, bespectacled man came up and quietly said, "Mr. Turner, I want to share my mission statement with you. I think it meets your test. It really helps me every day to get *my* head screwed on right and to motivate me, and it's only three words—"God-honoring change." I thought, *Wow! That's what mine is trying to say!* Here I was telling them how to do it and I didn't have it nailed down nearly as well as he did. He had captured the essence of my mission statement in a distinct and memorable way. He elaborated, "In every unique circumstance, with whatever persons are involved, I think, 'My mission here is to make the unique change, which honors God, and that's what I'm motivated to do.'" It was one of those cases when the trainee had gotten it better than the trainer. I presented *good* and he gave me back *great*, and I chose to follow his lead. "God-honoring change" has been my personal mission statement ever since.

QUESTIONS FOR REFLECTION

1. Are you open to learning from those who work alongside or "below" you? Name a person who is not officially your teacher or supervisor from whom you have learned much.

2. Do you find it difficult to share control over decision making? What about sharing credit for your team's accomplishments?

3. Does your communication style express to others that you value their input?

CHAPTER 5

FOLLOWING FAILURE

A life spent making mistakes is not only more honorable but more useful than a life spent doing nothing.

George Bernard Shaw

If there is one place where all of humanity can find common ground, it is in the experience of failure. Dig under the surface of even the most successful people and you will find lessons learned in defeat. Each of us has made mistakes. All of us have regrets. Why, then, are we so shocked, so stern with ourselves and others, when we slip and fall? Failure is as certain as death and taxes. All fail and fall short of the glory of God. All stumble along the journey of life.

We have seen how self-knowledge can help guide us toward a sense of mission, and we have seen what it means to work with others in a true spirit of collaboration and respect. We now come to that part of the journey where we deal with the inevitable—the times when we fail.

Failure is the gap between the ideal and the actual, between who we are and who we strive to be. "For I do not do the good I want," Paul said memorably in his letter to the Romans, "but the evil I do not want is what I do." Hitting short of the mark seems to be built into the fabric of being human.

When we think of failure, we often think of moral failure, and that is certainly a worthwhile place to start. Hardly a day passes without a news report of someone in business, religion, education, or government who has slipped and fallen. Whether it's the president telling the country that he lied about a sexual affair, the CEO of Enron being convicted of fraud and sentenced to prison, or an evangelical Christian leader getting caught in the underworld of sex and drugs, people fail morally. People do not simply break the Ten Commandments; they are broken *upon* them again and again. These foundational laws for societal survival are similar to the law of gravity. They can be debated, tested, and challenged; but the results are always the same—the law prevails, and we humans never seem to learn from the countless generations that came before us. It has been true since King David, intoxicated with power, came to believe he owned the rights to another man's wife and was willing to cover up his affair by killing his lover's husband. When we lie, cheat, steal, covet, and commit adultery, we damage our own souls and betray those who trust us. None of us sins in isolation; our transgressions hurt others, and these examples remind us that professed faith is no insulation from moral failure. Bill Clinton was a Bible-toting Baptist. Ken Lay was a church-going Methodist. Ted Haggard pastored one of the largest congregations in America and led a powerful organization of evangelicals. We can hide behind the Secret Service, our secretaries, our pulpits, or our vestments, but our sins have a way of being exposed. When we feel invincible, let us beware, lest we fall.

Not all failures are moral, however, and the process of following failure requires that we look at all its forms. There are situational failures, in which events and conditions overwhelm individuals, families, businesses, churches, and even nations, causing great loss and suffering, and chipping away at the foundation of a leader's confidence. Children can be overwhelmed when families, which exist for the purpose of providing safety, stability, affirmation, and love for all their members, are warped by dysfunction. God created marriage and family for noble and holy purposes, but tough situations can lead to courses of action that carry us far from the intentional will of God. Divorce can be the *circumstantial* will of God, who will continually work for our ultimate good, but our failure to make important relationships last is nonetheless devastating to everyone involved. The loss of a job can be due to economic factors, rather than personal shortcomings, but it is still a blow to our sense of self-worth as well as our financial stability. Natural disasters, health crises, the needs of elderly parents, and many other situations can turn smooth waters into raging rapids, both financially and emotionally. Following the lessons learned and the opportunities presented by situational failures can lead us to unexpected benefits.

Physical failures are a fact of life as well, knocking constantly at our doors, intruding at times like uninvited yet persistent visitors. We have an accident or suffer a heart attack. We develop cancer or Alzheimer's disease. Bodily functions we normally take for granted suddenly or gradually fail to operate. Few of us who reach old age get there with all our body parts. We lose teeth, get knees or hips replaced, and perhaps even lose a limb along the way to accident or a disease like diabetes. Our internal and sense organs weaken as degeneration flaunts its power in the face of our feeble attempts to hold it at bay. In the midst of such obvious frailty, we feel weak and vulnerable.

Can we avoid these physical failures? Maybe, somewhat, partially, for a while! We can eat right. We can avoid the use of tobacco and the abuse of alcohol and other drugs. We can exercise and socialize in appropriate measure. We can pray and worship, activities that are proving to be solid contributors to good health. Still, we are not masters of our diseases or captains of our health. We have inherited faulty genes. We breathe polluted air and drink chemical-laced water. All of us have a terminal illness called death.

DRAWING GOOD FROM THE BAD

Given the inevitability of all our failures—moral, situational, physical—we must learn how to face them if we are to live well or productively, and if we are to follow them toward a better future. In the practical sense, to follow failure means to do the next right thing as we begin to move on. To follow failure means learning its lessons, putting its pain and hardship to use toward building character. It means incorporating those lessons into the skills of leadership. It also means allowing failure to refocus us on our mission. When we do, failure can be one of life's most empowering influences.

The practical is always underlain with the spiritual, and it is there that we can see, even in the biggest failures and tragedies, the seeds of restoration. Faced with failure, where we cannot change what is, we must learn acceptance; but we must also begin the process of being made whole again. It begins with the grace of God, the unearned, unconditional, unending love of God for all people. It is a part of God's eternal willingness to have us be whole, to have us reunited in fellowship with God and those around us. If we have the courage to respond to that grace, we can walk a path that will bring us back toward healing, toward reconciliation. People of power and influence need to hear this message more than anyone: it is okay not to have it all figured out.

Grace was made for people who mess up and have the guts to admit it, something that is not always easy to do. Sometimes it is simply a matter of self-righteousness. It's easy to feel that our faults and failures are miniscule compared to what's reported on the news every day, so it can be hard for us to realize that we can't fix the matter ourselves. But, in fact, we stand in the same need of grace as the worst criminal in the dankest prison in the world.

Grace does not cure our cancers, correct our faults, transform our businesses, turn our children into model citizens, or guarantee we will get it right the next time around. Grace is rather the merciful hand of a loving God inviting us to follow our failures far enough to learn from them and start again. When we have failed on Formulas 1 through 408, grace is the courage to give it one more try.

How do we embrace this grace God so freely gives? It begins with **honesty** and **humility**. We call it *confession*. This is not the confession, all too common these days, that blabs its secrets in public for personal gain. Confession is owning our faults, mourning our losses, and acknowledging our pain as we look realistically at our own roles. Refusal to take responsibility for our mistakes is the biggest single impediment to learning from and rebounding from failure.

Blame and guilt are part of the normal processing of failure that takes place in society, but they are counterproductive to our attempt to follow failure toward something better. Finger-pointing and blaming others when all or some of the fault is ours is the surest way to get stuck in a problem, to let resentment swallow up the energy that might have been used for righting wrongs. Denial can't cure anything. Anger will not allow families to recover from destructive behavior. Blame will not get a business back on track. Success has many parents, but failure is an orphan. When we address and accept mutual responsibility for struggles and setbacks, we can move forward uninhibited. If we can adopt this sometimes humbling but always freeing tactic, we will have broken through. Once failure is owned, it is well on its way to being solved. In the church or in the corporate world, this is the point at which the group can get back to the business of repairing damage or setting its sights on the next challenge.

Honesty with ourselves and others puts us in a position to make a turnaround. We call this **repentance**—the biblical word is *metanoia*, which means to change direction. Following failure often means taking a U-turn on the road of life—we are not likely to reach our desired destination by traveling faster in the wrong direction. That means changing habits, changing behaviors, changing mind-sets. It is not easy to alter company policies or personal tendencies, and there is never a convenient time to make an adjustment in spending habits or our level of physical activity. We do not change directions because we want to. We change directions because we have to.

Repentance leads to **forgiveness**, which is not a right to be earned but a gift to be received. Forgiveness is not a reward for hard work—it is a gift of God. All forgiveness starts with God's forgiveness of us. God's forgiveness leads us into self-forgiveness. This is tricky because people too often see self-forgiveness as simply forgetting they ever messed up. Self-forgiveness first means owning the fact that we are fallible, feeble, faulty, frail human beings. We are capable of great accomplishments, but we are likewise capable of causing ourselves and others a great deal of pain and grief. Like

Pogo, "We have met the enemy and he is us." Unlike "I'm okay. You're okay," the truth is this: I'm not okay. You're not okay. And that's okay.

Once we face the reality of our brokenness, however, we must find a way to start again, to be reconciled not only to God and ourselves, but to others as well. Personal forgiveness leads to relational forgiveness, which is the oil that lubricates the human machine. That's not to say it's easy. "I was wrong, I am sorry" may be the hardest six words in the English language. They stick in a man's throat. They cause a woman to blush. They make a child run and hide. But sorrow over our past failures can deepen us and equip us for a more successful future, as twentieth-century poet Robert Browning Hamilton said in his poem "Along the Road":

> I walked a mile with Pleasure;
> She chattered all the way,
> But left me none the wiser
> For all she had to say.
>
> I walked a mile with Sorrow
> And ne'er a word said she;
> But oh, the things I learned from her
> When Sorrow walked with me.

Forgiveness empowers **restoration**—one of life's finest words. It means to reconstruct, rejuvenate, repair, refresh, renew, revitalize, reinstall, reinstate. Remember how David said it in the world's most beloved Psalm? *"He leads me beside the still waters; he restores my soul"* (Psalm 23:2-3).

Restoration gives us the chance to use the talents of people who might be otherwise lost to us. Why should we throw away the brightest minds in the world because they happen to inhabit bodies that refuse to be controlled? Why should we label people relational failures because they stumble in marriage? Are people who falter in the face of some strong temptation, who fail with their family or finances or fret over some physical illness, damned for all time? I don't think so. Jesus talked about forgiving seventy-times-seven times and, given human history, it is clear that God's capacity for forgiveness is infinite. It is the possibility of learning from our mistakes, of being forgiven and restored, that enables us to follow our failures, big and small, toward more effective and gracious leadership.

WHAT FAILURE CAN TEACH US

While no one would or should volunteer for faults and failure, there are lessons to be learned at the University of Hard Knocks that are not part of the curriculum at other schools of life. Among the things to be learned from trouble are these:

There is strength to be found in weakness. The Bible says that when we are weak, then we become strong (2 Corinthians 12:9). This apparent paradox is borne out in practice, for weakness is a great teacher, and its lessons can strengthen us. Weakness forces the body and soul to become receptive to the ministrations of others, and it can generate living proof that people really will care for you when you cannot care for yourself. What a relief!

There is acceptance to be found in surrender. There is an amazing freedom that comes when we stop pretending that we have it all together. Surrender is more than resignation. It is different from giving up. Acceptance does not mean that all the questions are answered. It does not refrain from asking, "Why?" Surrender puts us in touch with our human limitations. There are things we can change. There are things we cannot change. If we have the wisdom to know the difference, we will discover the joy of letting go.

Perseverance is an antidote to despair. People in trouble can easily lose hope. When we are embarrassed at our frailties and humiliated by our struggles, hope is to the soul what oxygen is to the body. Hopeless people die not from disease but from despair. We do not have to like the pain, but persevering through it will help us follow our failure to a more hopeful future.

Character refinement leads to a life of compassion. Success may teach us competition, but failure teaches us compassion, something in which most of us could use a lesson or two. It is easy to judge. It is tempting to condemn. It is self-satisfying to compare. But it is loving to care. It is kind to understand. It is empowering to forgive. Dealing with others who fail, we would do well to maintain some of the humility, some of the compassion and community we are sure to learn in our own dealings with failure and restoration.

These lessons, applied to our lives, can have a huge impact. We will no longer be able to simply discard leaders who fail morally as we might abandon a wrecked car that once carried us reliably. Nor will we write ourselves off as potential leaders because of past failures. We will look for the ways to mend broken families and to welcome all in community. We will not ignore the needs of those who are marginalized and invisible, for when we fail to hear the cry of the needy, we sin against God and our neighbors. We will follow Jesus' example when it comes to those who are crippled or lame, those who are HIV-positive, those struggling with cancer. In the face of weakness, of brokenness, of failure, we grasp that remedy of restoration, which does its powerful redemptive work when grace works through us.

Most of the time we have little say about what happens to us. But we have everything to say about what we will do with what happens to us. So never let a trouble go to waste. Let trouble be your teacher and failure be your guide, and let it teach you grace, compassion, and love. That is how we can best follow our faults and our failures toward greater personhood and stronger leadership. It is possible to discover that there is health after sickness, life after divorce. People do recover from bankruptcy and criminal charges just as they do learn to live and even thrive with cancer. And if other people can do it, so can you.

FROM THE DESK OF
CAL TURNER JR.

My upbringing brought me plenty of "failure management assets." The influence of my mother was a big help. "Son," she used to say, "for a good boy you get into a lot of trouble." That was a beautiful separation of the person from the teenage crime. It taught me that I am not the failure; the failure is separate from me. It's a healthy way to deal with it, and it positioned me for the rest of my life to have a little bit of humor in the face of failure and to seek a healthy ego separation so that I could better learn the lessons failure held.

My struggle with the role of boss's son enabled me to think through the prospect of failure before I ever started my career. I knew that success would not be attributed to me because my position had been handed to me. Failure, on the other hand, would be fully blamed on me for the same reason. As much as that scenario seemed to put me in a lose-lose situation, though, it turned out to be a rare advantage, a career-positioning philosophy that helped me in major ways throughout my business life.

One of the lessons I have learned is that in the aftermath of failure, guilt and blame are counter-productive. At Dollar General, we aimed for an environment that did not involve either one. We tried to process "gaps" between the ideal and the actual in ways that would develop the person and the team, always keeping in mind that if you get beyond blaming others, you empower everyone to learn as much as possible. When something goes wrong, the quickest way to engender defensiveness is to say, "Who did that?" One difference in management styles between my dad and me involved that question, and it may have been simply a generational thing. He would say, "Who did that?" I would say, "Daddy, I'm not even going to tell you who did it, but let me tell you this. There were several 'whos.' Any time something goes wrong, there are several contributors, but I won't have us lay primary blame on any person except me. I'm the leader."

Whatever goes wrong is vested in the leader, if he or she is a true leader, one who accepts the blame and dispenses the credit to others. I remember shocking our CFO when the company was in trouble because we had made acquisitions we shouldn't have made and with bad timing. I made the statement that I, as leader, accepted the blame. That was part of my role. He was aghast. "Why should the leader accept the blame?" he asked. "Because," I said, "that is what leadership is all about." It empowers an organization. It lets the air out of the "blame bubble" to have a leader who says, "I accept it all."

In a sense, my career was defined by failures and their lessons. Early on, there were the inevitable failures inherent in learning how to get relationships right. Business development is about relationships, and because of the stress involved it is even harder to have good business relationships than good relationships with friends. Later, there were failures that stemmed from bungling tactics or strategy as we undertook rapid growth without sufficient technological or staff support. Then there were failures that stemmed from the difficulties of adding new management as the growth continued. Finding the right person for a specific job and bringing him or her in to work alongside your existing talent is a very difficult undertaking, and failure is part of the process now and then.

Each of those failures helped me to grow and allowed the company and the people in it to take the next step forward. Perhaps the biggest failure, though, came at the turn of the century, and it could have dealt a fatal blow to my entire career. A few months after my father died in November 2000, Dollar General had to restate its financials because of the discovery that they had been wrongly reported. There is no way to overstate the importance of that event. The credibility of a public company lies in its financials, the bottom line it reports to its shareholders, and ours was on the line.

One of my failures as CEO was making our incentive and bonus compensation structure too dependent on our bottom line. Earnings per share determined the bonuses and stock options of everyone from assistant store managers all the way up to the CEO. In a 6,000-store chain, that is a lot of people. Each year, the board set targets, and attaining those targets determined whether or not *everybody* got rewarded. In my mind, it was a powerful and empowering thing to do. It was the ultimate statement of our being in this as a team. And yet, it put such emotion-laden, gut-churning pressure on people to achieve that number that some good people did things that were wrong.

Once we began investigating the full extent of the problem, we had to alert the Securities and Exchange Commission, which set in motion a dramatic and very public chain of events. While this procedure was necessary, the process designed to doctor the patient can often kill it. The agenda of necessary forensic accounting and legal investigations adds a major financial cost and can just take the heart out of a company, particularly a company that is so dedicated to its people, its customers, its employees, and its values. I believe a company with a more harsh management style would be more able to withstand the stress of financial restatement, but the people-centered, values-centered dynamic that made Dollar General successful could potentially have resulted in company implosion.

When the Dollar General restatement was first announced, some people said, "Well, it's obvious they were cooking the books." Now, that hit way below the belt of someone who's been a values-based leader. A longstanding shareholder was quoted as saying, "It feels like my beloved dog has died." As a shareholder, he felt Dollar General was that wonderful, and when you're deemed wonderful and you foul up, you suddenly become worse than bad.

My deepest processing of the mistake occurred between me and my Father in heaven, as my earthly father was no longer alive. I was thankful that this event had not occurred while my dad was here to witness it in person. Our conversations came back to me, though, because here was Cal Jr.'s ultimate test regarding the blame-free leadership style he had advocated to his father. But Cal Sr. was dead now, and Cal Jr. faced a major temptation to ask, "Who did this dastardly thing? How did this happen?" My test was to follow through on what I had always said was the right response to failure, and in this case it involved extricating myself from the management of Dollar General, enabling the company to reconstruct its future without Cal Turner Jr.

At the end of the long legal process, my victory was in not having to face the typical CEO plight of being officially banned by the Securities and Exchange Commission from serving as an officer or director of a public company, as frequently happens in response to a restatement of company financials. I use the term "victory" loosely, since the absence of a major negative is hardly a positive worthy of great celebration. The relief I felt at avoiding that public stamp of disapproval was bittersweet because of my consistent and long-standing emphasis on values in leadership. Nonetheless, I was determined to follow my failure toward new opportunities for leadership, benefiting others in my community, my church, and in higher education.

The SEC investigation did lead me to some unexpected blessings in retirement. Someone whose identity is too deeply engrossed in business (especially the family business) is going to have great difficulty in retirement because he can never actually make that major shift of gears. The failure I felt during the SEC investigation helped me make the transition to a successful life after Dollar General.

FROM THE DESK OF

J. Howard Olds

Most of my life, I have taken great pride in being physically strong and mentally tough. I love competitive sports, and I often channeled that same drive into church growth. Challenges are opportunities to shine, and the bigger the challenge, the greater the spotlight when the job is done.

I first became aware of the biggest challenge I would ever face on January 2, 1997. I had spent the day before watching ballgames and developing strategies for the church I was privileged to serve. I rose early to prepare for a breakfast appointment, and when I stepped out of the shower I noticed a lump under my right arm. "I'd better lighten up on those driveway basketball games with my sons," I thought as I went off to work.

A few days later, the lump was still there. A visit to my internist led to a CT scan, and two days later I underwent surgery to remove cancerous lymph nodes. Three weeks after that I started chemotherapy. Six doses of potent drugs and two-dozen radiation treatments later, I thought I had conquered the failures of my body. For the next six years I was free of any signs of cancer.

Then, in the summer of 2003, I started feeling ill again. After a number of tests, I learned that the cancer was back. This time I underwent a stem cell transplant, something my oncologists told me would take me to the door of death and bring me back again. "Was it necessary to dangle me so close?" I asked them jokingly when it was over.

Once more, though, I recovered. I learned to cherish the word *remission*. In 2004, however, the cancer was back again, this time in my brain, requiring surgery and a second regimen of chemotherapy. A year after that, it came back again and attacked my abdomen, pressuring my kidneys and heart. After a couple of false starts, we found a chemotherapy that worked, and again I heard that marvelous word "remission." Months passed. We traveled, enjoyed our grandchildren, and cherished every breath.

Then, in 2007, another routine scan revealed even more shocking news. There was more cancer, this time in the colon. I went through another surgery.

For ten years, now, I have followed the failures of my body toward a better understanding of perseverance and surrender. I have learned to accept the kindness and help of others. After years of being the minister, the strong one, I have had to learn to let others do for me—in all sorts of ways.

For one, our congregation has showered my wife, Sandy, and me with expressions of genuine love, support, and care—verbalized, written, and acted out in various ways over and over again. People from other churches I have led, back to the first two tiny ones in Kentucky, have sent e-mails, cards, and messages of hope. Little children, five and six years old, grab me each Sunday and say, "Dr. Olds, I pray for you every day." That network of people, constantly bombarding us with words of affirmation and love, create a sense of community beyond what I knew was possible. And with every return of the cancer, this community's love and care pours forth even more intensely.

Then there is the way my wife has reacted. She and I married at eighteen, so we've been together forty-three years, and she has become a fabulous soul mate. Our struggles have created a depth in this relationship that neither one of us have known before—it's more honest, open, and supportive than ever; and it's amazing to see her role change. She's not the upfront or gregarious one. She was the schoolteacher, with her own world and her own profession. But when I get sick, it's almost like she goes through a personality change. She takes charge. She'll negotiate with doctors and work with hospital nurses and deal with church members who fail to understand our need for privacy. She's like a sergeant. And it's the same thing with me: "You take your medicine now," she'll tell me. We laugh about it. It's amazing to see her new personality when I'm weak. That could be a source of trouble in some relationships; but, boy, it's been a comfort. I can lie here doubled up, on Oxycontin, praying I'll get through the day without feeling too much pain, and she can run the show. That's been a tremendous help. The same thing has been true with our two sons, who want to know how they can help and who will also ask, "How are you *really* doing?"

In God's hands, physical failure can deepen relationships and make us stronger and more loving. That is not to say it's easy. At this point, I am not a cancer survivor. I am a cancer warrior. I go to war with it daily. The battle will not be over until these bones of mine are buried. But although I may have cancer, cancer will never have me.

QUESTIONS FOR REFLECTION

1. How do you handle failures, crises, and disappointments?

2. How would practicing repentance and forgiveness help you move past difficult circumstances you face?

3. Think of a setback you've experienced recently. To what opportunity is this failure leading you?

CHAPTER 6

FOLLOWING CHANGE

In times of change, learners inherit the Earth, while the learned find themselves beautifully equipped to deal with a world that no longer exists.

Eric Hoffer

Eventually, we will all know the feeling. We may be like the young man who visits the lake house of his childhood. He climbs the hills and walks along the river where life was once an adventure worthy of Tom Sawyer. But things seem different now. The islands are not as big as he remembers them. The hills are not as steep. The journey seems shorter. The hills and river have not changed. The boy has changed.

Or we may be like the couple taking a casual drive past the first home they shared as newlyweds. Businesses now line the highway that then wound through open countryside. Subdivisions and shopping malls have replaced cornfields and pastures. Their quaint neighborhood now appears overgrown and run down. Eventually, one says what both are feeling: "My, how things have changed!"

Most of us like to reminisce about life the way it once was. We all have our "glory days" that we remember fondly—our time on a college sports team, the fun-filled years when our children were young, or a particularly exciting period in our career. If we are honest with ourselves, however, things were not really so perfect back then as we imagine they were; and we would not be very successful individuals if we had not progressed beyond those eras.

Change is the natural order of things, and—whether willingly or reluc-tantly—all men and women, companies, churches, communities, and countries encounter it continuously. Corporations face new competition, new markets, new generations, and new tastes and trends among their cus-tomer base. Churches face new social movements, changing demograph-ics, competing congregations and ideologies, new demands on people's time and energy, and the increasing secularization of society. Communities and nations face swelling or dwindling populations, diseases and natural disasters, violence and terrorism, and a host of other challenges. Each of us faces a constantly changing world, the eventual loss of friends and family members, and, of course, a day-by-day journey that leads to that most final and universal change—death. Change is necessary. Change is constant. Change is inevitable.

Change is also quite often resisted. Growing as an individual or an or-ganization is in part learning to deal wisely and effectively with the con-tinuous onslaught of change. It might seem reasonable to embrace that process as a path to maturity, strength, and wisdom; and yet it's obvious that many of us resist. We seem inclined to prefer established practices to radical reformations, and those of us who may desire change are hesitant to challenge those in power who wish to preserve the status quo. "If you want to make enemies," said Woodrow Wilson, "try to change something." True innovators, who push boldly into new territory despite opponents and naysayers, seem to be vastly outnumbered by those content to stay where they are.

At the top of any list of institutions that resist change you will find churches. Nowhere are you more likely to hear, "But, we've never done it that way before." Churches chafe at the new longer and adapt to it more slowly than any other service agency. There are reasons for this—some more valid than others. Churches are not driven by the profit motive. While more people mean more money and more money means more min-istries, many churches are not willing to adapt their style and facilities enough to have broad appeal in this ever-changing consumer society.

Churches—especially small churches—are usually controlled by strong-willed laypeople with decision-making power, and all too often their decision is to resist change at all cost. In some denominations, judicatories continue to fund dying churches when they can no longer fund themselves, rather than risk upsetting long-time members by closing or merging congregations. Dead churches litter the landscape of city and countryside alike, because no church officer wants to sign the death certificate and no pastor wants to hold a respectful funeral service. Clergy become little more than chaplains for these hospice-type situations.

ADAPT OR PERISH

While self-preservation techniques may seem inviting on the surface, they prove disastrous in the long run. Like the fragile human body, the body of Christ will cease to function if dramatic measures are not taken to repair and adapt when necessary. The same is true of corporations and other agencies—all are rife with people vested in doing things the old way, and all will die without willingness to change.

Dynamic organizations, however, have leaders willing to embrace change and follow it toward new life. Ideally, change agents are imaginative, daring, determined, passionate leaders who intentionally frame a clear, compelling vision of what needs to happen. They will do so in such a way that people welcome or at least accept the new direction. Let's examine how the effective leader will handle the stages of change.

The first step is often the most difficult, as many leaders struggle to **recognize the need for change**. Acknowledging that change is the normal state of affairs is a great beginning. In most cases change is not something we undertake willy-nilly in the midst of calm and prosperity. We should change neither out of boredom nor simply because everyone else is changing. Rather, intelligent change is our response to the prod of events and circumstances in constant flux. Most change is simply a reaction to what has already happened. The leader who follows change does not so much establish the need for change as understand and recognize that need as it presents itself. "What changes, what new conditions are we facing?" the leader might ask. "What do they mean to us and what should our response be?" Good leadership takes a clear-eyed look at the organization's place in a world in constant motion. It is also clear on the status of the institution itself. So the first question change agents must address is, "Why?" Changes have to flow out of purpose, vision, and mission. Why does a particular company exist? How does it plan to serve its customers? Churches would also do well to constantly reevaluate their purpose for existence. If the purpose of a church is to make disciples, the failure to produce any new disciples for decades is reason enough to consider change. If the church's neighborhood has changed radically over the last twenty-five years, how can a congregation justify business as usual? Change is not a question of convenience, satisfaction, or even cost. Change is determined by need and is driven by the commitment to meet such need.

Change is facilitated by **making a plan**. Part of the reason many people are resistant to change is fear of the unknown. If they have no idea where they are being led, they are not very likely to follow. Plans make change more predictable and more manageable. The ancient saying about eating an elephant is profoundly true. You take it one bite at a time. People are more likely to take the first step if they have some vision of the final destination. Change agents know how to paint a picture in such a way that even nonvisionary people can grasp the idea. Herb Mather wrote a witty little book called *Don't Shoot the Horse 'Til You Know How to Drive the Tractor*.[1] In it, he asserts that like mid–twentieth-century farmers, churches and businesses must find new methods to meet desired goals. New challenges require new means of operation. We cannot be content with obsolete tools, but we also cannot abruptly abandon them without a plan for their replacement. Develop a new plan, make sure everybody is on board and at least moderately comfortable, and *then* let go of the old ways. Such planning helps avert disaster and gives naysayers more time to adjust to necessary changes.

It is important to **reach consensus** in the process of facilitating change. People are much less resistant to change if they feel it is not being imposed upon them autocratically. They do not resist change so much as they resist *forced* change, or change whose outcome is uncertain. People are much less likely to resist change that has clear benefits or rewards. Consequently, the change agent must take the time to develop the art of building consensus. Answer questions. Make adjustments. Listen to resistance. Explore alternatives. Followers of change use every possible means of bringing people together. They do not, however, acquiesce to stallers, manipulators, gossipers, or people who simply object to everything. There is an old story about a community newcomer who encountered an old-timer at the neighborhood coffee shop. As the two gentlemen pursued a friendly conversation, the newcomer said, "I bet you've seen a lot of change in this community over your lifetime." The old-timer took another sip of coffee and replied, "Yep—and I am proud to say that I have been against every bit of it." There are people who are simply born in the objective case. They object to everything. Change agents give such people a voice, but do not indulge them with veto power.

In the best sense, to be an agent of change is to find what is good in the present and seek to make it better. Presented that way, it is an exciting proposition. People will want to become part of that dynamic if they are invited. They are less likely to be resistant to change if they anticipate that change to have a positive outcome.

That brings us to another critical aspect of facilitating change, one we've already emphasized as a crucial part of responsible leadership: **communicate, communicate, communicate**. Despite the fact that many of us have cell phones, Blackberries, e-mail, and fax machines, we are very poor communicators. We don't put across the relevant information at the appropriate time, and we are not good listeners. When there is a chain of command, careless communication up or down the ladder can call to mind the childhood game Telephone, where you whisper a sentence to someone who passes it on until it's often changed beyond recognition. And there are subtler problems. Communication can have layers, and it's important to relay them all. Sometimes we get across all the right facts but leave out the context, which can make or break the resulting action. Sometimes we confuse commands with communication—the latter involves valuing the other person's understanding, which will improve the quality of the implementation. Skimping on communication in the interest of saving time is seldom a wise move.

Of course, sooner or later effective followers of change have to **take the plunge**. After developing the plan and building consensus through clear communication and deliberate discussion, leaders must face that lonely moment of decision, then take action. Sometimes there is good reason to hold off on a choice, but often we face critical moments in which failing to decide is in itself a decision to fail. We can hesitate about making up our minds, but we cannot hesitate about making up our lives, for our lives get made up one way or another. We are always seeking more input, but the nature of change is such that we will always be acting on partial information. There comes a time when we accept the fact that we cannot know or understand everything, and we act on the information available. In a world of constant change, to do nothing is to be left behind. Change is always to some extent a leap of faith.

There will still be naysayers in the wings. There will be supporters in the background. Some people will not have an opinion one way or another, but boldly following change requires calling the shot, taking the leap, making the decision, and assuming the responsibility that comes with it. Here is where much change falters. There will probably be people angry with the person who pulls the trigger. The decision itself might be faulty. Some things will not be known until they are tried. Leaders who follow change are willing to take these risks. The rest sit around and complain.

If making a decision to act would put an end to change, all leaders could rest a little easier. Of course, such is not the case. In the aftermath of a decision, it is important to **evaluate and adjust**. Nobody gets it exactly right on the first try. Mid-course corrections are as essential in business as they are in space flights. New information becomes available. Participants with some experience under their belts can better evaluate what is working, what isn't, and why. Such evaluation and adjustment are critical. Then it is time to assess the outcome of the action. What was good and what was bad about the decision and its aftermath? Such analysis is important because further decisions will be waiting down the road.

Change involves a creative chain of events. It is a continuous process. Change demands continual flexibility and a willingness to admit failure. So, followers of change keep looking, listening, stopping, altering, and doing whatever else is necessary to reach the intended results. That is why change agents must have enough self-confidence to change again and enough perseverance to hang in there.

That leads us to a final point. **Change must not be laid in concrete.** Some people who facilitate great change fall in love with the change they facilitate. They lose their objectivity. They become defensive. They fail to realize that all change will lead to further changes. What serves us well today will most likely become obsolete tomorrow. So, major companies go public, then they go private, only to go public again. Churches open themselves to social events only to discover in time that they have become community centers with only a tinge of spirituality. Sometimes we get what we want and then discover that we did not want what we got. But within that uncertainty lies the very hope that change supplies. We are not chained to the changes we engineer. Further changes can make things even better, or clean up the mess we made by the changes we instigated.

Followership is tested and proven in its reaction to change. If you are a leader and nothing is different from when you took over, then your legacy is one of impotence, not importance. The opportunity to change is one of the great gifts life offers. It can be the antidote to failure, the path to increased knowledge and wisdom, the way to better service and deeper relationships. Handled poorly, it can spell destruction; but handled wisely with sound principles, it can turn our potential into actuality and yield untold benefits.

FROM THE DESK OF

J. Howard Olds

Churches, like people, can be defined by their acceptance of or resistance to change. Pastors, congregations, even entire denominations ebb and flow as they react or fail to react to the dynamics of the world around them. It might be instructive to look at the stories of two United Methodist churches that share Middle Tennessee locations and illustrious histories, but far different fates.

The first was founded early in the nineteenth century by a group of Methodists who migrated west from North Carolina after their leader received a land grant. The trustees read like a Who's Who in the Methodist Church at that time and the new church flourished. One account says that more than a thousand people attended a protracted meeting at the church. But the church was not on a river, a highway, an Indian trail, a railroad, or even a buffalo path. In time, the population shifted and the church declined, kept open by old families who remained in the community. Finally, in the 1960s, the church, still standing on its original one-acre site, was closed by the Tennessee Annual Conference. Because of its historic significance, it was reopened a few years later under the jurisdiction of the History and Archives Commission of the Tennessee Conference of The United Methodist Church. Now surrounded by multimillion-dollar homes that came with the surge of large subdivisions into the area, the little clapboard church continues to be served by a full-time Elder of the Conference who ministers to a small handful of the faithful. Not far away, a new town began developing in the 1850s. It was called the Village of Brentwood. Town leaders

felt the new community, located on a railroad and two turn-
pikes, needed a church. When they could not persuade existing churches to relocate, a couple of them decided to start a
new one. They bought two lots and built the Brentwood
Methodist Episcopal Church, South. The church struggled
some during the Civil War, but eventually began to grow and
develop. In the 1880s, plans to move the church nearer the developing population center were accelerated by a tornado. The
church thrived in its new location. In the 1930s lightning
struck the church, which burned to the ground. It was rebuilt
on the same spot. In the 1970s Nashville, Tennessee, surged in
population, and the city of Brentwood grew as a suburb of the
Nashville metropolis. More people migrated to Brentwood, and
the community changed rapidly. Office parks, developed next
door to the church, housed the headquarters of some of America's major medical corporations. The church again faced a
crossroads, and once more its leaders made a positive decision
to move, this time a few blocks south on a major highway providing space to expand and serve the community. In 1972
church members marched down Franklin Road to their new
campus. In the early 1980s they made major additions to those
facilities, and in the early 1990s purchased more property and
built an 1,800-seat sanctuary. In 2002 they purchased still
more land and built a ten-million-dollar Discipleship Center
with a state-of-the-art youth facility, day school and day care
space for children, well-equipped conference rooms, and a
banquet hall used by the community as well as the church.
Brentwood United Methodist Church now has more than 6600
members. It offers five varied worship services each weekend
and has developed a reputation for outstanding youth and children's ministries in the community. This is the church I have
been honored to serve for the past eight years, and I am excited for the future of this dynamic congregation.[2]

The difference between these two United Methodist churches
lies in a single word—change! One decided not to change with

the times. The other saw change as an opportunity. As one fifth-generation member of our congregation succinctly states, "As Brentwood changed, Brentwood Methodist Church changed with it." I credit the church's continued growth to flexibility in two main areas: leadership and worship.

Brentwood Church has never had a senior pastor serve for more than ten consecutive years. In fact, the church has been served by 51 senior pastors over its 155 years of existence. That represents an average stay of only three years! One characteristic of many large-membership churches today is the presence of a long-term pastor, one whose tenure might stretch for twenty-five to forty-five years. Such longevity provides stability. It also produces anxiety and sometimes chaos when an inevitable change in pastors finally comes. Brentwood Church, however, watches pastors come and go, each with individual strengths and abilities. Meanwhile, the church continues to pursue its vision of touching hearts and transforming lives.

Brentwood Church has also demonstrated a willingness to shift worship styles and explore new avenues of service to the community. Mainline churches can easily hemorrhage over debates regarding worship styles. Replacing a pipe organ and hymnal with a band and video screens often leads to more screaming than singing among the faithful. On the other hand, questioning the theology or methodology of contemporary worship likewise meets resistance. I am amazed at how out-of-place and shunned a person can feel who dares to walk into a laid-back worship service dressed in a suit and tie, and drinking something besides Starbucks coffee. America's worship wars are still raging, but Brentwood Church has maneuvered on this battlefield in effective ways, facilitating change while honoring traditions. The congregation has provided a wide menu of worship opportunities including traditional worship, emerging worship, contemporary worship, and blended worship. Dress varies from three-piece business suits to blue jeans. The latest wave of change is a move toward multiple campuses to meet the needs of an ever-changing population.

No one of these provisions is unique in itself. It is the process that deserves consideration. Change is inevitable, but leaders who follow change can successfully guide their organizations to vibrant futures.

FROM THE DESK OF
CAL TURNER JR.

My father and I had a great deal of love and respect for each other. He was a people-loving person, and he made no bones about his admiration and respect for me when I came to work for him. He was very proud of what I'd accomplished to that point—graduating cum laude (which I couldn't even pronounce until May of 1962) from Vanderbilt University and serving for three years and four months in the Navy—and he was eager to turn the family business over to his number-one son. That didn't mean, though, that the process was going to be easy. Change almost never is, and our strong personalities made the transition even more difficult.

We were largely unaware of our own competitive juices and how they would come into conflict with each other. My dad was a dynamic entrepreneur, and although he had a heart as big as the outdoors for people, he was an intense man and his word was law. I was no shrinking violet myself, and I still had some of my Navy rough edges around me. I was single at the time, and I had moved into my parents' house for a while. The room and board were great, but the situation intensified our relationship. We were playing bridge one night with my mother and one of her friends; and my dad, in his own Type-A way, was being pretty aggressive, teasing and heckling me as we played. He was probably unaware that his competitive streak was so fully engaged. I took it for a while, but then I looked at him pointedly and, cleaning up the Navy language considerably, said, "Would you get off my butt?"

It was as if the earth had stopped. Very little could stun my father into silence, yet I had just done it! He was as shocked and upset as I had ever seen him; he looked as though he was about to cry and, seeing that, I wanted to cry. He folded his cards and set them down. We all did the same. It was obvious the game was over.

I'm not sure to this day why my words affected him so strongly. I guess they seemed completely out of character for me, since this was probably the first pushback he had gotten from me as an adult, and he wasn't accustomed to any pushback at all. Yes, I had toned down the language; but in the Turner family home in Scottsville, Kentucky, those words from son to father were simply unacceptable. It was clear that becoming colleagues in the business was changing our personal relationship as well.

The four of us, the house, our whole world, became frigid. It wasn't any warmer the next morning. I knew I was going to have to do something. My plan was to approach him at work and render an apology with strings attached, the way most people do. I'd say I was sorry and tack on some qualifications and make it clear I expected him to apologize back.

He and I had the only two offices in the company at the time. Mine was in one corner of the upstairs warehouse, and his was in another. He had an executive washroom, and when I got there, he was in it. I was relieved, because that meant I could apologize through a closed door. I stood outside and started talking, wrapping it up after a while with a fervent, "And so, Daddy, I'm sorry."

There was dead silence . . . for a long time . . . long, awkward, dead silence, worse than the one that had descended on the card table the night before. I stared at the door, from behind which there was nothing forthcoming. Finally, he said, "Son, I accept your apology." He let that sink in for a moment and then said, "You know, Son, in any successful relationship, there has to be flexibility. However, in a father/son relationship, I don't think anyone should expect the father to be flexible!"

What in the dickens can I make of that? I thought. I walked back to my office.

I may not have understood it then, but that statement of my father has stuck with me to this day. Flexibility is vitally important when it comes to dealing with change. In times of change, the healthiest person is the one who expects himself to be flexible but who minimizes his expectation that others will be flexible in return. Some of my greatest difficulties have come when

I've expected life or other people to be flexible. Sometimes they aren't; and when I keep expecting them to be, I'm bound to be disappointed. The world is filled with curmudgeons, zealots, and tornadoes, people with agendas and just plain ordinary people having bad days. All of them taught me the value of flexibility—mine. When I set aside what I perceive as their responsibilities in a situation, I can focus on my responsibilities and do what I need to with greater empowerment.

Bringing me into Dollar General meant major changes for the company, for my father, for me, and for our relationship. We had to begin relating to each other on a man-to-man level rather than just on a father-and-son or boss-and-subordinate level because we were jointly running a big business. We needed to move toward something closer to equal footing. It was a process that continued throughout my father's life, and it was not always smooth sailing. I learned over and over the importance of being flexible, and of letting him be who he was.

Change can be threatening; but if we don't fight it, it can be one of the key components in our growth and development as persons. Cultivating inner flexibility is our best shot at taking air out of the "blame bubble" and helping change to work for the greater good. If we have that flexibility, if we learn accommodation, if we expect little from others and remain thankful for the good things in life, we can deal with change. In fact, we can deal with almost anything.

QUESTIONS FOR REFLECTION

1. How do you usually respond to change?

2. What steps of following and facilitating change are hardest for you?

3. How are you currently being challenged to be an agent of change in your organization?

CHAPTER 7

FOLLOWING THE UNKNOWN

Be patient toward all that is unsolved in your heart, and try to love the questions themselves like locked rooms and like books that are written in a very foreign tongue. Do not now seek the answers, which cannot be given you because you would not be able to live them. And the point is, to live everything. Live the questions now. Perhaps you will then gradually, without noticing it, live along some distant day into the answer.

Rainer Maria Rilke

It is human nature to ask questions and seek answers. Learning by asking is part of the adventure we have been on since the day we were born. Take a stroll with any child and the questions fly: "Why is the sky blue? Where does the sun go when it sets? How do birds know to fly south for the winter?" Children innocently trust that the adults in their lives have the answers to their questions about the sun and the sky (and eventually about the birds and the bees).

Then children start asking tougher questions: "Why did we put Granddad in the ground if he went to heaven? My playmate up the street is dying of cancer. Does that mean I am going to die? If God is real, why can't I see him?" Suddenly, adults are not as omniscient as they once seemed, and we seek answers from a wider variety of sources. We expect science to explain the vast complexities of the universe, and trust it to cure our diseases. We pursue religion for answers to age-old questions about our purpose and the nature of a human soul. Answers to (or at least a million people's attempts to answer) these questions are now as close as our personal computers, thanks to the information superhighway. With the ubiquity of cell phones and PDAs, we have become accustomed to getting in touch with others the very moment we need to talk to them. We have been spoiled by our instantaneous access to information to believe that every question has a clear and easily available answer. Even when it comes to the "mysterious ways" in which God purportedly works, many of us just can't wait to figure them out. How many times have you heard someone say, "When I get to heaven, I'm going to ask God . . ."? Like sixth graders peeking at the answers in the back of their math books, many of us can't bear one day of not knowing if we've figured things out correctly, much less a lifetime of pondering the unknown.

Though it runs counter to our nature, embracing the unknown is essential not just to our sanity but to our souls. What would the journey of life and leadership be if we knew up front how it would all end? Who would God be if humans could comprehend him? It's hard to accept this when even religious institutions that wrestle with deeply existential questions succumb to the temptation to explain life's mysteries. Churches market themselves as places to find answers to difficult questions, when some of life's most significant questions do not have answers. There are some things we will never understand. People faced with this reality can become cynical and conclude that the world is untrustworthy, or they can learn to live the questions.

Living the questions is not merely resignation to the unanswerable. It is searching, wondering, hoping, asking, and following the unknown without the urgency to find the final answer. It is trading security for integrity and certainty for faith. It is living with our fears in such a way that they evolve into the hope that things can be all right even when they are all wrong.

ASKING THE TOUGH QUESTIONS

Such a mindset is most challenging when we try to make sense of the troubles we all inevitably endure in life. Even in light of modern medicine and the wealth of certain nations, we struggle with the question, "**Why do people suffer?**" The question is as old as Job and as current as the evening news. Rabbi Harold Kushner attempted to answer the question in his popular book *Why Bad Things Happen to Good People*. The book contains the moving story of Kushner's struggle to understand the loss of his fourteen-year-old son to progeria, a rare disease that drastically speeds up the aging process. He spends seven chapters analyzing and disputing popular assumptions about good and evil (for example, that God sends hurricanes or house fires to punish people who have done wrong). But in the end, Kushner finds no clear answer, determining that while God is good, bad things happen regardless of our virtue.

The ancient book of Job tackles the same question. Job loses not just a child, but everything—family, possessions, wealth, and health. Friends come to comfort him in his misery, only to make matters worse with their pat answers. Job's wife advises him to "curse God and die." But Job is not about to give up so easily. So he goes straight to God with a lifetime's worth of "Whys," but God will have none of it. God reminds Job that his human brain could not comprehend the answer even if God tried to explain it. So the riddle of human suffering continues. Faithful followers learn to live the question.

Closely related to the question of suffering is the personalization of pain. When suffering strikes, the question, "**Why me?**" finds its way into our hearts. Sometimes our religion even complicates the matter. In 2006, a Comair flight out of Lexington, Kentucky, crashed at the end of the runway, killing forty-nine of the fifty people aboard. A young mother of two was scheduled to be on that flight. At the last minute, she changed her departure time in order to be with her children a little longer. As people of faith, that young mother and her family praised God for saving her life, but the rejoicing raised several questions. What about the forty-nine people who died? Were they not living in the favor of God? Did God give them a warning they failed to heed? Was there a reason they perished and she didn't?

In a *Ziggy* cartoon, Tom Wilson deals with the "Why me?" question this way: "Whenever I ask, 'Why me?' a voice always says, 'so who else did you have in mind?'" One way to handle the "Why me?" question is to replace it with the question "Why not me?" It can help put things in perspective to realize that we are no more or less deserving of suffering than anyone else.

Another everlasting question is **"Why do wrongdoers prosper?"** It was a favorite of the psalmists. Psalm 73:12 (NIV) says, "This is what the wicked are like—/ always carefree, they increase in wealth." A person we'll call Henry was in his early forties, trying to make a living and raise a couple of kids. He would not consider himself to be a saint, but he did try to do an honest day's work for an honest day's pay. He said his prayers and took his family to church on Sundays. He didn't cheat on his expense account, and he valued his customers enough not to gouge them for extra profit even when they might not know the difference. Still, making a living selling business forms is hard work. The competition is tough. And the district manager always seemed to expect increased sales with fewer resources. One day Henry leaned across the table of a neighborhood restaurant and confided in a trusted friend that playing fair in business had become a disappointment. Henry was no longer confident that honesty was the best policy. It certainly appeared that people who padded their expense accounts and took advantage of their customers were faring far better financially than he was. There may not be a businessperson or pastor alive who has not pondered the questions Henry was asking that day.

People do not always reap what they sow. They do not always get what they deserve. It rains on the just and the unjust. The lottery gods are no respecter of persons. Swindlers prosper, and even after being caught, they often find a way to swindle again. Just as bad things happen to good people, sometimes good things happen to bad people. We do not know why, but we can follow this question to find a greater motivation for living an ethical life.

Sometimes, amid inexplicable suffering, we ask, **"Why is God silent?"** Theologian C. S. Lewis speaks for millions of grieving people when he writes in his book *A Grief Observed* these poignant words: Why is it that "when you are happy, so happy that you have no sense of needing [God], . . . you will be—or so it feels—welcomed with open arms[?] But go to [God] when your need is desperate, when all other help is vain, and what do you find? A door slammed in your face, and a sound of bolting and double bolting on the inside. After that, silence."[1]

How long, O Lord, how long? How much, O God, how much? Are you there, Almighty, are you there? These are the prayers of those struggling along the journey of life. When these prayers are met with silence—deadening silence—our hope as well as our faith is tested.

What is success? The answer to this life question becomes more elusive as the years go by. When one is a novice in business or the ministry, the nature of success is often clear and easily defined. Success means establishing yourself as a competent person capable of taking responsibility and making wise decisions. In the early years, success means moving up the company ladder or increasing church membership. It is catching the attention of superiors and having them regard you as a person with promise. Success is usually measured by bigger sales, larger pastorates, greater influence, and larger salaries. While the functions of business and church appear to be radically different, the measurements of success are amazingly similar. There comes a time, however, in both church and business when even the so-called successful begin to question their success. They climb the ladder but gradually begin to wonder if the ladder is leaning against the right wall. They reach the top only to discover they have become sitting targets for jealous wannabes more than ready to replace them. Slowly we come to realize that success is a moving target. Such realization calls for reassessment and more questions.

The questions are endless, but for our purposes, maybe one more is enough to consider: **What on earth am I doing for heaven's sake?** This is the question of significance. It flows out of our definition of success. It confronts us with the reality of our mortality. And it narrows our narcissism enough for us to take our place with the endless line of others who have had their moment on the stage. We are not immortal. We will not be remembered forever. So how can we do what we can and give what we have in the little time we have to live and give? The biblical understanding of our earthly purpose is one of stewardship. We are not owners. We are renters. "The earth is the LORD's, and the fulness thereof," says the psalmist (Psalm 24:1 KJV). While no two of us have the same gifts and graces, or even equal resources or opportunities, we are all accountable for what we have done with what we have been given. Is this not the meaning of the powerful parable of the talents told by Jesus? Some have one talent. Some have two. Some have more. As the story goes, the one-talented man was timid and afraid, so he hid what he had in hope he would at least break even. The two- and five-talented people were different. They took a risk. They invested. They ventured. They doubled their assets. Judgment day came. The investors were praised for their investments. The insecure one was condemned for his carefulness. Was Jesus advising people on the stock market, or are the stakes much higher? When the bell rings at the end of the day, what will we have done with what we have been given?

THREE THINGS WE CAN KNOW

If the unknown is a fact of life, what can we be sure of in this world? That powerful trilogy of the Apostle Paul comes to mind: "And now faith, hope, and love abide, these three; and the greatest of these is love" (1 Corinthians 13:13). These are the virtues that we can trust, and they can help us combat despair as we strive to follow the unknown.

"Faith is the substance of things hoped for, the evidence of things not seen," says the Bible (Hebrews 11:1 KJV). Faith is the bird that feels the light while it is still dark. What kind of faith does it take for us to feel light through darkness amid the questions and struggles of our lives? Some faith is born of certainty. God shows up in mysterious ways and makes his wonders apparent. Things work out. Life comes together. Miracles happen. Such victories make our faith strong. Not all faith, however, is laced with great evidence and filled with inspiring revelation. Some faith must be grounded in trust. When God is silent, when no miracle happens, when the cancer returns, when the kid goes wrong, when the business fails, when the church declines, we must trust that God will be with us every step of the way. Trusting faith sees the light before the dawn. Three things sustain us through the questions, and the first of these is faith.

Hope is akin to faith but a little different. As the theologian Emil Brunner suggested, hope is as essential to the soul as oxygen is to the body. People die without hope like people die in deep coal mines when methane gas replaces oxygen. It is important to recognize that hope is more than just positive thinking. A prisoner of war was asked how he survived years of imprisonment in the Hanoi Hilton concentration camp. The prisoner answered with one word: hope. The same prisoner was asked about those who failed to survive the horrible ordeal. Who were they? Again the prisoner answered with one word: optimists. Optimists kept predicting they would be released by Christmas, by Easter, by Independence Day. When those holidays came and went, the optimistic prisoners fell into despair and died. Hope is different than optimism. Optimists say, "Cheer up! It could be worse." When things do get worse, though, they have no recourse. The hopeful, on the other hand, never give up. Against all odds they keep believing, keep living, keep pushing on. The hopeful persevere into the unknown, confident that good will ultimately prevail.

"Faith, hope and love abide, . . . and the greatest of these is love." Love is more than a romantic notion or a heartfelt emotion. Love is fundamental respect and good will toward God, toward others, and toward ourselves. If the world could ever replace its love for power with the power of love, we might all be saved. Love meets our deepest human hunger. The unknown does not seem so frightening when love is present.

Consider, for example, how doubts and questions can overwhelm couples who are just beginning their journey together: *Do I really love this person? Can I tolerate his quirks? Why is she so moody? When will he be home? Why is she late? What will other people think?* After a while, if love grows into commitment and attainment deepens into acceptance, questions lose their urgency and the cross-examinations fade. Doubts have not all been resolved, but have just been absorbed by love.

We are human and we desire certainty, but certainty is not part of the human equation. That truth becomes even harder to handle when it comes to the truly important things in life. We may grumble, but most of us can take it when the car breaks down or the parade gets rained on. It gets tougher when friends disappoint us or when opportunity slips away. It is then that we rely on people we trust to reassure us. Hardest of all are those uncertain situations that shake us to the core. Loved ones die. Mates betray us. We face catastrophic illness. Suddenly the consolations of friends and ministers can flow by without effect, and we can feel utterly and desperately alone.

But there is another truth of human existence, one at once more elusive and more real. Through the centuries, it has brought strength to the weak and courage to the dying. It has kept believers moving forward a step at a time, singularly and in communities. It allows one person to minister to another when it takes the strength of both just to move forward. When it doesn't have answers, it has at least a hand to offer. This is often the essence of followership—leaders looking beyond their own status and objectives to serve others and strive for the good of all. This kind of leadership knows that nearness can be more important than words, and that love trumps knowledge. It seeks and nurtures a sense of divine purpose, and acts out of humility and compassion. It is clear about direction, but aware that life is more journey than destination.

It is somewhere within that combination of faith, hope, and love that we find the power that has changed lives for millennia. Though it is not always explainable, it is always available, provided, of course, that we avail ourselves of it. Even doubt cannot negate this power. In fact, there are times when it is better to step forward in doubt than to hesitate in faith. There may be gaps in knowledge, but we must keep moving, ever venturing to take the next step in a journey of meaningful service.

Take that step, uncertain and faltering though it may be. Follow the unknown, and find your way home.

FROM THE DESK OF
CAL TURNER JR.

One of the toughest periods in Dollar General's history came at a time when we had over-expanded and found ourselves in unknown territory. We were in trouble and had to ask some very tough questions: "Why have sales and earnings gone to pot?" and "What went wrong with the new stores?" We had added 50 percent to the size of our company in about fifteen months and didn't have the infrastructure to support what we were already doing, much less the new growth we were taking on. (It's amazing how things that seem so obvious in hindsight were so imperceptible at the time!) We simply were not doing a good job of merchandising in new markets different from those in our Kentucky and Tennessee base.

Behind these questions, however, was a bigger one I wasn't yet asking—a question of leadership. Actually, it was more than just leadership—it involved family. Dollar General, though a public company, was in reality a family business being run as a public company, and now the stress of rapid growth was going to demand that we resolve some family issues.

Merchandising—turning cash into merchandise your customers want, at the right quantity, price, and presentation, and turning that back into more cash—is the primary asset movement of any retail company, and it was also the prime mover of a Turner family dilemma. My brother and I shared management of the company. I was chief executive officer, and he was chief operating officer. Although he directed merchandising, I had the ultimate responsibility for merchandising as well as all other company functions. Our differences came to a head when my brother advocated far fewer changes in merchandising than I as CEO considered essential. My mandate as CEO was drastic change throughout the company. After months of deep brotherly soul-searching, I told my brother that the needed change had to begin with merchandising, and that it might therefore be necessary, considering our disagreements, for him to step down from merchandising or maybe even leave the company.

"Well, then," he said, "there's a bigger change required here, Brother. I'm not going to resign. You're going to have to fire me."

Could I really fire my own brother? It was a question I hated to ask, with unknown consequences I was afraid to face. But I had to ask it. I had to. *I have to be willing,* I thought, *to accept the responsibility of asking the question that could break up our family, but that employees, customers, and shareholders of our public corporation required me to ask as CEO.*

The pain and stress of that question literally drove me to my knees. I was struggling, crying inside. I needed help. I needed guidance.

Everybody needs someplace to go when he doesn't have the answer, when the right response is beyond him. I went to my God and to the book that I hadn't read nearly as often as a good Bible-belt Methodist should. But in the face of that crisis, my reading of the Scripture became one of crying inquiry. I read intently, and I found the conviction I needed in the fifteenth chapter of John: "I am the true vine, and my Father is the vinegrower. He removes every branch in me that bears no fruit. Every branch that bears fruit he prunes to make it bear more fruit." That went to the heart of the matter. Between two brothers, there was inadequate fruit, and significant pruning was required. I had to take ownership of that, and my brother actually helped me to do it!

Dollar General was a three-ring circus of sorts, led by the company's founding entrepreneur and his two sons, brothers whose different perspectives resulted in sibling rivalry we could not get past. We wanted to do different things with the company. It wasn't my fault. It wasn't his. But the joint vision the company needed simply did not exist. I knew the company needed one fully positioned CEO. That was a fact in the best of times, and it was especially true with a company in trouble, as ours was. I also knew that I was the person, and that it was now a matter of stepping up to being that person. I was going to have to assume full responsibility; if there was cutting away to be done, I was going to have to do it. Ultimately, my brother exited the business, but he did so gracefully, and both the company that our father founded and our extended Turner family are strong today because of that grace.

There were consequences for that difficult action, but I learned that good can come out of what seem to be the most impossible circumstances. Ironically, if Dollar General hadn't gotten into trouble by over-expanding and hurting its performance as a public company, I might never have had to address some of the hard questions that eventually led to a much stronger and ultimately much larger public company. Dollar General may well have failed amid family squabbles rather than reaching new levels of success. Instead, this change in the family business improved both the business and our family. The relationship between my brother and me became more grounded in mutual respect as a result of the major trauma we faced together. Larry Appley was right in saying that human relationships and joint creativity flourish when grounded in mutual respect. Except as found in the Good Book itself, that may be, for me, one of the best definitions of genuine love.

Following the unknown is seldom a straightforward proposition. There are all sorts of twists and turns, elements and motives and layers we can't see going in. Following the unknown takes courage. It takes openness. It also takes grounding in God that can give us a firm place to stand even when all around us is changing.

All of us—individuals and corporations alike—will face questions that lead us into the unknown. They can come from friend or foe, in good or bad times. The process can be as painful as it is important. Facing those questions can involve a great deal of soul-searching, and it will more than likely be difficult. But following the unknown to the lessons it holds for us is our highest quest under God.

FROM THE DESK OF
J. Howard Olds

Not long ago I woke in the middle of the night, short of breath, and I started to panic. "I wonder if this is what it's like to get to the end and die," I thought. I don't live with questions about the afterlife. I may have some theological concerns, but I have genuine faith that it's there, and I think it's going to be better than here. I think it's going to be just and fair. But the process of dying frightens me to my very core.

The physical part of that night was nothing more than indigestion. I was eating primarily vegetables because of my upcoming colon surgery, but that night I'd had a crab cake for dinner. I shouldn't have done it, but it sure was good while I was eating it. So I took some Rolaids and they, indeed, spelled relief. But I had to ask myself, *What was going on in your brain and your soul that suddenly made you so anxious over a brief shortness of breath?*

A couple of nights after that episode, Sandy and I had a conversation. We've learned to turn off the TV more, and she's no longer teaching school and having to get up early in the morning, so we can take time to talk. I told her about the indigestion and then about my fear of that moment—when you're trying to get your breath and it's not there, and you're thinking about what the end will be like. I said, "I'm scared about that. I'm just scared to death about it."

I have no idea what heaven is like. I don't even try to figure it out. But I do believe in it because if there is a God, which I choose to believe there is, this thing called life just doesn't make sense if there isn't an afterlife. That's the only way I can assume some kind of justice exists. I just buried a twenty-nine-year-old who had spent the last twenty-six months of his life battling leukemia. At the funeral service I said, "If there's not something out there, it's not only a cruel world, but you've got a cruel God." Then I met with a group of his friends to talk through their grief, to discuss the tragedy of the circle of life getting cut short. In your thirties you're supposed to be trying to live, not trying to figure out immortality.

Still, I said to Sandy, "If you and I are just all wrong about this, if there's no such thing as God and human life is nothing more than animal life so that when we're dead we're dead, I'd still live the same way. It's been a great trip, and I wouldn't change anything." There is peace in that, and no need for bitterness. I've chased all the dreams I need to chase. I enjoy living. I want to live every minute I can, but when it comes to compromised living—and I deal with the doctors on this all the time—I tell them, "Don't do something to me that's going to compromise my ability to function. I'd rather be dead than spend the time I have left lying in a hospital feeling awful." That's not living, in my book.

Cancer is now a constant reality in my existence, but I'm not ready to die or give up. Being able to step into the pulpit on Sunday morning, being able to guide this church or to visit somebody who's dying, that's the best therapy I can get. I feel like I'm doing something meaningful, and the people around me who can be totally honest assure me that I'm still making a meaningful contribution. That alone enhances the quality of my life. I consider it a great honor and privilege.

When it comes to working with people who are dying, the key is not giving them answers. It's letting them raise the questions and letting them know they're not abandoned. You lay their hands in the hand of God. I don't have as many answers as I did when I was thirty, but I still find it tremendously meaningful to walk with people through the valleys and shadows of death. I wouldn't want to do anything else, thankfully.

And now it is my situation, my walk. The thing that has bothered me mentally and emotionally now is this: I've done this war with lymphoma for more than ten years, and now they run scans and find colon cancer. It's not even lymphoma extended to the colon, but a totally unrelated cancer. I've got the same colon cancer my mother died of and the same lymphoma my father died of. One cancer would have been plenty. This new diagnosis leaves me with certain questions: Is this thing all hereditary? And if so, how did I get it while three of my siblings didn't get any of it? Still, I don't dwell too much on the "Why me?" question.

I've got my nice theories about suffering. Some we bring on ourselves. Some others bring on us. And sometimes, in the human body in the natural world, the system just doesn't work. There's too much rain or too much drought. I don't think God wills any of this on us, and miracles are a complete mystery to me. I see them happen once in a while, but I don't think if I prayed harder or got a bunch of people to pray that I would be healed. It's simply in God's hands. I don't blame God. I don't feel like God cut me short. Rather, I feel the strength of God, the presence of God.

Sometimes, I can reach back toward my own childhood and feel that presence. Growing up, I'd go to that little church in Kentucky three times a week and sing. Gospel songs are all we ever sang—songs like "Blessed Assurance" and "Just As I Am." I've got four or five meditation CDs full of those songs, and I can tell you, I know all the words to them. Now and then I just crank up that music and listen, and I find peace in that. It goes all the way back to the good parts of my childhood, and it always helps me feel the presence of God.

Still, what I don't know is greater than what I do, and I think perhaps there's a wild card. I like what Lewis Smedes says. What if, before you're born, the Lord said, "I don't have this life thing all figured out. Sometimes it's not going to be fair. There are going to be some rough spots. Do you want out? Do you want to be born, or do you want to skip it?" What would you answer? Would you take the risk of being born into this troubled world?

There's no doubt in my mind—I'd go for it.

QUESTIONS FOR REFLECTION

1. Are you uncomfortable with questions that don't have clear answers?

2. What unanswerable questions do you wrestle with most?

3. Are you currently walking in "unknown territory"? Will you let the Unknown drive you to despair, or will you follow it to a life of adventure, courage, and hope?

CONCLUSION

We live in a world that cries out for good influence on every level. Responsible and ethical leadership is as essential as oxygen in every context from the family dinner table to the legislative chamber, and yet it seems we know leadership best from its failures rather than its successes. Those failures are seldom matters of incompetence, but rather of ego. They are failures of integrity and character—in short, failures of self. Leadership requires something more than self-propulsion. True leadership, we have seen, requires the ability and willingness to follow something greater than ourselves.

Sometimes the mission is monumental in an earthly sense. War, political and economic turmoil, scientific and technological achievement, racial and ethnic equality all call for the kind of leadership that makes headlines and history books. More often, the mission is small in an earthly sense but important in a larger spiritual sense. How do we impact our families? How do we influence our small circles of friends and acquaintances? What sort of tone do we set at work and at play? What kind of outlook do we bring to the little conversations that make up the bulk of our daily discourse?

The people around us are affected by everything we do. Our presence changes the world in good ways or bad, and that direction is a simple matter of how we lead in the broadest sense. The tone we set in the smallest settings carries over into the larger arenas we enter. "Whoever can be trusted with very little can also be trusted with much, and whoever is dishonest with very little will also be dishonest with much" (Luke 16:10 NIV). We can't forget about integrity and character in our day-to-day dealings and expect to be moral giants in times of crisis. We can't expect to reflect Pharaoh day in and day out and channel Moses when it counts.

We know the big problems—armed conflict, poverty, crime, a thousand forms of personal and societal weakness and dissolution. And we know what we are called to do: feed the hungry, clothe the naked, visit the imprisoned. In short, love God and our neighbors. Our leadership grows out of those imperatives.

The process starts as we align ourselves with that calling, as we find the highest possible mission and internalize it. It continues as we seek the best in others, as we draw on and encourage their strengths. It flourishes as we deal constructively with change and turn challenge, heartache, and failure into fruitful resources as we regroup, find forgiveness, and move forward. It is there that we move from being islands of self-absorption toward lives integrated in pursuit of an ultimate purpose.

Heed the call. Follow your true self to a life of meaning. Follow your purpose and serve others with your talents. Follow others to a truly collaborative approach to life's challenges. Follow change and failure toward new strength and perspective. Follow the unknown, seeking to walk in love and faith when knowledge proves elusive or inadequate.

You will not have far to look for the chance to lead and inspire. The world is a place in need of all the love and leadership we can give it. Opportunity lies in every person who struggles with shortcomings and life's inequities, in every situation that proves to be a stumbling block to someone. Apply these principles in your own life and you will be able to share them, at first haltingly, and then with more assurance, with others. And it is in doing so that we live out our true missions, to bring light to the world as our own gifts and circumstances allow.

NOTES

1. Following: A New Understanding

1. Edgar F. Puryear Jr., *American Generalship: Character Is Everything: The Art of Command* (Novato, Calif.: Presidio Press, 2000), 229.

2. Following the Person Inside

1. Henri Nouwen, *Life of the Beloved: Spiritual Living in a Secular World* (New York: Crossroad Publishing, 1992), 30-31.

6. Following Change

1. Herb Mather, *Don't Shoot the Horse 'Til You Know How to Drive the Tractor* (Nashville: Discipleship Resources, 1994).
2. Taken in part from an unpublished article by Vance Little.

7. Following the Unknown

1. C. S. Lewis, *A Grief Observed* (New York: Bantam Books, 1976), 4.